CONTRIBUTIONS
TO
ENGLISH LITERATURE

CONTRIBUTIONS

TO

ENGLISH LITERATURE

BY THE

CIVIL SERVANTS OF THE CROWN

AND

EAST INDIA COMPANY

From 1794 to 1863:

WITH OCCASIONAL BIOGRAPHICAL NOTES

LEOPOLD CHARLES MARTIN

GYAN

Published by

Gyan Publishing House
5, Ansari Road
Daryaganj, New Delhi-110002
Phone: 011-47034999, 9811692060
E-mail: books@gyanbooks.com

Distribution Network
gyanbooks.com
India, USA, Canada, UK, Australia

ISBN: 978-93-7225-717-5 (PB)

First Published, 1865

2nd Impression 2025

Printed at: Gyan Press, Delhi.

CONTRIBUTIONS TO ENGLISH LITERATURE
Author: LEOPOLD CHARLES MARTIN

CONTRIBUTIONS

TO

ENGLISH LITERATURE.

CONTRIBUTIONS

TO

ENGLISH LITERATURE

BY THE

CIVIL SERVANTS OF THE CROWN

AND

EAST INDIA COMPANY

FROM 1794 TO 1863.

WITH OCCASIONAL BIOGRAPHICAL NOTES.

BY

LEOPOLD CHARLES MARTIN

OF H. M. STATIONERY OFFICE.

1865.

TO

THE RIGHT HONOURABLE

WILLIAM EWART GLADSTONE, M.P.

CHANCELLOR OF THE EXCHEQUER

ETC. ETC.

THIS VOLUME IS INSCRIBED

AS A TRIBUTE OF THE HIGHEST RESPECT

BY

HIS MOST OBEDIENT SERVANT

LEOPOLD CHARLES MARTIN.

H. M. STATIONERY OFFICE:

1865.

PREFACE.

IT was formerly much the fashion to represent the Government Official as a species of sinecurist, whose chief occupation was to solve the difficult problem, how to dispose of the brief hours of service required by the Treasury Minutes; and although of late years their merits have been more justly appreciated by the public, comparatively few are aware of the very important services rendered to the State by the Civil Servants of the Crown and the East India Company, entirely independently of their duties and exertions in an official capacity. The object of the following work is to supply this information in a simple and concise form; and to thus show that, so far from being overpaid and underworked, some of the noblest names in every branch of English Literature, and some of our most laborious authors, have been in the official employment of the Government; while it is the fame of the labours of their leisure hours which has in many instances made us forget the unobtrusive routine of their Official Services.

I am not aware that any attempt has hitherto been made to furnish a collected list of the contributions to English literature by the Civil Servants of the Crown and the East India Company, and I venture to crave indulgence for defects almost unavoidable in a first essay at such a compilation. Although I have availed myself of every means in my power to collect the titles of the various works, and to ascertain the dates of the publication of the first editions, it is to be feared that the Catalogue will still be found very far from complete; and I therefore would fain hope to be favoured with any information which may enable me to correct errors or repair omissions should a second edition be required. One great difficulty has been to decide where to commence, but the necessity of limiting the size of the book has led to confining the Catalogue to the works of those who have been officially employed since 1794. Nevertheless, the works mentioned were in numerous cases published during the lifetime of their respective authors and long prior to that date. Should my present effort be received with sufficient favour to enable me to issue a second series extending to the reign of Elizabeth, I need scarcely observe what bright names in British History would be comprehended in the list.

In the present work the Biographical notes have been compressed to the smallest compass; and to afford facility of reference a double index has been added, the first portion of which comprises the names of the various authors, and the second portion the names of the official departments in which they were employed. A cursory glance at these lists will show how numerous and distinguished are those whose literary labours identify them with the industrial classes, including as it does such names as Burke, Burns, Godwin, Charles Lamb, Cornewall Lewis, Macaulay, McCulloch, Mackintosh, Henry Mackenzie, Wordsworth, &c., &c., who have been taken from us, and Brougham, Gladstone, Earl Russell, Bulwer Lytton, Disraeli, Layard, &c., &c., who are still spared to advance the cause of progress. A perusal of such names cannot fail to excite feelings of deep respect and gratitude to those who have devoted themselves so entirely to the services of their fellow-countrymen.

HER MAJESTY'S STATIONERY OFFICE:

March 1865

INDEX OF AUTHORS.

INDEX TO DEPARTMENTS.

Science and Art.

Secretary of State, Colonial.

Secretary of State, Home.

Secretary of State, Foreign.

INDEX TO EAST INDIA COMPANY,

NOW

DEPARTMENT OF SECRETARY OF STATE FOR INDIA.

CONTRIBUTIONS

TO

ENGLISH LITERATURE.

ADAIR (Right Hon. Sir Robert, G.C.B. M.P.)

Office of Secretary of State, Foreign Department.

Born May 24, 1763. Educated at Westminster School, and at Gottingen. Elected M.P. for Appleby in 1802; for Camelford in 1806. Early in the same year appointed Minister at the Court of Vienna. Employed in 1808 on a special Mission to the Sublime Porte: created a K.C.B. on his return. Was Ambassador at Constantinople from 1809 till 1811. And again employed on a Special Mission to Belgium in

1831. Retired from the public service in 1835 Died October 3, 1855.

Published

An Historical Memoir of a Mission to the Court of Vienna in 1806. 8vo. 1844.

A Memoir of the Negotiations for the Peace of the Dardanelles 1808–9. 8vo. 1845.

On Organisation of the Military Forces of Great Britain. 8vo. 1855.

Various Political Pamphlets.

ALCOCK (SIR JOHN RUTHERFORD, K.C.B.)

Department of Secretary of State, Foreign.

Born in 1809. Educated at the Grammar School at Capheaton, and studied in the London hospitals. Acted as surgeon in the Spanish Legion from 1833 to 1837. Appointed a Commissioner for the settlement of the various claims of the British Legion from May 1839 till 1844. Appointed Consul at Foo-chow-foo in 1844; at Shanghae in 1846, and at Canton from 1854 till December 1858. Was nominated Envoy Extraordinary and Minister Plenipotentiary and Consul-General at Japan in November 1859. Created a C.B. in 1860, and K.C.B. in 1863.

Life's Problems. 8vo. 2nd edition. 1862.

Medical History of the British Legion of Spain. 8vo. 1838.

The Capital of the Tycoon, or Narrative of Three Years' Residence in Japan. 8vo. 1862.

ASHBURTON (LORD), ALEXANDER BARING.

Board of Trade.

Born October 27, 1774. Conducted for some time, in the United States, the American branch of the mercantile house of Baring Brothers, and became head of the firm in 1810. Represented Taunton in Parliament from 1812 to 1820, and Callington from 1820 to 1831, and North Essex from 1832 till 1835. Became President of the Board of Trade under Sir Robert Peel in 1834. Raised to the Peerage in 1835. In 1842, at the instigation of Sir Robert Peel, appointed Special Commissioner to the United States to settle the Maine Territory Boundary dispute; the result of which was the Ashburton Treaty.

An Inquiry into the Causes and Consequences of the Orders in Council and an Examination of the Conduct of Great Britain towards the Neutral Commerce of America. 1 vol. 8vo. 1808.

BANDINEL (JAMES).

Department—Secretary of State, Colonial.

Some Account of the Trade in Slaves from Africa, as connected with Europe and America, from the Introduction of the Trade into Europe down to the present time. 1 vol. 8vo. 1842.

BARROW (SIR JOHN, F.R.S.)

Admiralty.

Born June 19, 1764. In 1792 appointed Comptroller of the Household to Lord Macartney in his Embassy to China. Became Private Secretary in 1797, when his Lordship was Governor of the Cape of Good Hope, subsequently and till the year 1803 was Auditor-General of Accounts at the Cape. Appointed by Lord Melville, in 1804, Secretary to the Admiralty. Created a baronet in 1835, during the administration of Sir Robert Peel. Retired from the Admiralty in 1845. Died November 23, 1848.

Travels in China. 4to. 1804.

Voyage to Cochin China in the years 1792–1793, &c. 4to. 1806.

Life of Lord Macartney, with Selections from his unpublished Writings. 2 vols. 4to. 1807.

Chronological History of Arctic Voyages. 8vo. 1818.
Life of Lord Howe. 8vo. 1837.
Life of Lord Anson. 8vo. 1839.
Life of Lord Drake. 8vo. 1844.
Memoirs of Naval Worthies, Reign of Elizabeth. 8vo. 1845.
Life of Peter the Great. 18mo. 1846.
Autobiographical Memoir. 8vo. 1847.
Sketches of the Royal Society and its Club. 8vo. 1849.
Account of the Mutiny of the Bounty.
Numerous Articles on miscellaneous subjects in the Quarterly Review and the Encyclopædia Britannica, &c.

A'BECKETT (GILBERT ABBOTT).

Department of Secretary of State, Home.

Born in the year 1810. Educated for the legal profession at Westminster School. Called to the bar in 1841. First employ in the Civil Service in 1846, under the Poor Law Commissioners, to inquire into the condition of the Andover Union. Appointed a Magistrate at the Greenwich and Woolwich Police court in 1849. Transferred to the Southwark Court in 1850. Died on April 28, 1856.

Established in 1830, and edited, a satirical journal, the precursor of 'Punch,' entitled 'Figaro in London.'

The Comic Blackstone. 12mo. 1844.

Quizziology of the British Drama. 12mo. 1846.

The Comic History of England. 2 vols. 8vo. 1848.

The Comic History of Rome. 1 vol. 8vo. 1852.

Various burlesque pieces for the stage, produced during the years 1825–43.

One of the chief contributors to 'Punch' from its commencement in 1841 till 1856.

BIRCH (SAMUEL).

Keeper of Antiquities, British Museum.

History of Ancient Pottery and Porcelain. 2 vols. 8vo. 1858.

BOWRING (SIR JOHN).

Department of Secretary of State, Foreign.

Born October 17, 1792. First employed by Government in 1828 to examine into the method of keeping the Public Accounts Abroad; and again in 1831 as Commissioner to France, to arrange a Treaty of Commerce. In 1836 was a Commissioner to inquire into the Registration of Births, Deaths and Marriages in England and Wales. Elected M.P. for Kilmarnock in 1835; for Bolton in 1841 and 1849. Appointed Consul at Canton in 1849. Superintendent of Trade in China from 1852 till 1853. Knighted in 1854 and appointed Governor of Hong-Kong. Retired in 1859.

Specimens of the Russian Poets. 2 vols. 8vo. 1821–23.
German Lyric Poets. 8vo. 1822.
Batavian Anthology; or Specimens of the Dutch Poets, &c. 8vo. 1824.
Ancient Poetry and Romances of Spain. 8vo. 1824.
Servian Popular Poetry. 8vo. 1827.
Specimens of the Polish Poets. 1827.
Poetry of the Magyars. 8vo. 1830.
Cheskian Anthology, History of the Poetry of Bohemia. 8vo. 1832.
Minor Morals for Young People. 3 vols. 1839.
Decimal System, with illustrations of coins. 8vo. 1854.
Kingdom of Siam, with a narrative of a Mission to that country in 1855. 2 vols. 1857.
Visit to the Philippine Isles. 8vo. 1859.
Various Reports on Foreign Commerce. 1834–40.
Edited the Westminster Review from 1825.

BROUGHAM & VAUX (Lord Henry, D.C.L., LL.D.)

Lord High Chancellor of England.

Born in 1778. Educated at the High School, and at the University of Edinburgh. In 1800 admitted Advocate at the Scottish bar. Called to the English bar at Lincoln's Inn in 1808. In April 1820, appointed Attorney-General to Queen Caroline. Created Lord Chancellor in 1830: resigned in 1834. Represented Camelford in Parliament in 1810, Winchelsea in 1820 and 1826, and Yorkshire in 1830. Was Chancellor of the Edinburgh University in 1859. Created D.C.L., Oxford, in 1860, and LL.D. Cambridge, in 1862.

Collected edition of Works in 11 vols. 8vo. 1857-60.

Vol. 1, Lives of Philosophers of the time of George III.

Vol. 2, Lives of Men of Letters of the time of George III.

Vols. 3 & 4, Sketches of British Statesmen of the time of George III.

Vol. 5, Sketches of Foreign Statesmen of the time of George III.

Vol. 6, Natural Theology; Dialogues of Instinct, &c.

Vol. 7, Rhetorical and Literary Dissertations and Addresses.

Vol. 8, Historical and Political Dissertations.

Vols. 9 & 10, Speeches on Social and Political Subjects.

Vol. 11, The British Constitution.

BULLER (RIGHT HON. CHARLES, M.P.)

Poor Law Board.

Born at Calcutta in August 1806. Educated at Harrow School; at the Edinburgh University, and at Trinity College, Cambridge. Elected M.P. for West Looe in 1830, and for Liskeard in 1832. Appointed Private Secretary to Earl Durham on his Mission to Canada in 1838. Was Secretary to the Board of Control in 1846. Appointed Judge Advocate and Queen's Counsel and Member of the Privy Council, in July, 1847. Became Chief Commissioner of the Poor Law Board in November 1847. Died November 28, 1848.

Report upon the Affairs of Canada. 1839.
Poor Law Reports.
A Series of Papers on Responsible Government for Colonies. 1 vol. 8vo.
Various articles in the Edinburgh and Westminster Reviews.

BULWER (RIGHT HON. SIR HENRY E. LYTTON, G.C.B.)

Department of the Secretary of State, Foreign.

Born in 1804. Originally in the army: retired in 1829. Attached to the Prussian Mission in 1827; to the Austrian Embassy in 1829; to the Hague in 1830. Elected M.P., first for Wilton and then for Coventry in 1831. Attached to the Paris Embassy in 1832, and made Secretary of Legation in 1835. Represented Marylebone as M.P. from 1835 to 1837. Appointed Secretary to the Turkish Embassy in 1837, and Secretary to the Russian Embassy in 1838. Removed to Paris, and appointed Minister Plenipotentiary in 1839: remained till 1841. Was Ambassador to Spain from 1843 to 1848. Made Privy Councillor in 1845, and K.C.B. in 1848. Appointed Minister and Envoy to the United States in 1849. Removed to Tuscany in 1852, and to Constantinople as Ambassador Extraordinary and Minister Plenipotentiary, in 1858.

Autumn in Greece. 8vo. 1824.
France: Social, Literary, and Political. 2 vols.
Monarchy of the Middle Classes. 2 vols. 1834.
Life of Lord Byron.

BURKE (Right Hon. Edmund).

Department of the Paymaster-General.

Born January 1, 1730. Educated at the Classical School, Ballintore, County of Kildare, and at Trinity College, Dublin. Appointed Private Secretary to the Marquis of Rockingham when First Lord of the Treasury in 1765, and elected M.P. for Wendover; took his seat January 14, 1766. Returned M.P. for the City of Bristol, November 1774. Sworn a Privy Councillor, and appointed Paymaster-General of the Forces in 1782. Retired from public life in 1794. Died July 9, 1797.

Philosophical Enquiry into the Origin of our Ideas on the Sublime and Beautiful. 8vo. 1756.
Vindication of Natural Society. 1756.
Accounts of the European Settlement in America. 2 vols. 8vo. 1757.
Observations on a late State of the Nation. 8vo. 1769.
Reflections on the French Revolution. 8vo. 1790.
Correspondence between the years 1474 and 1797. 4 vols. 8vo
Thoughts and Details on Scarcity. 8vo. 1800.
Speeches. 4 vols. 8vo. 1816.
Epistolary Correspondence. 8vo. 1827.

BURKE (SIR J. B., LL.D.)

Office of Arms, Ireland.

Called to the Bar at the Middle Temple in 1839. Appointed Ulster King-at-Arms, November 1853. Knighted February 1854.

Authorised Arms of the Gentry. 8vo.
Dictionary of the Landed Gentry. 8vo. 1860.
Encyclopædia of Heraldry. 8vo. 1844.
Family Romance on Annals of Aristocracy. 3 vols.
Heraldic Register. 8vo. 1849.
Historic Lands of England. 2 vols. 1849.
Knightage of Great Britain. 1841.
Orders of Knighthood. 8vo. 1858.
Peerage and Baronetage. 8vo. Published annually.
Roll of Battle Abbey, annotated.
Romance of the Aristocracy. 3 vols. 8vo.
Royal Descents, Pedigrees of Founders of Kin. 8vo.
Seats and Arms of the Nobility. 4 vols. 8vo. 1855.
Vicissitudes of Families. 1st, 2nd and 3rd series. 8vo. 1859-62.

BURNS (ROBERT).

Excise Department.

Born January 25, 1759. Appointed to an office in the Excise in 1788. Died July 21, 1796.

Poems:—
1st edition, published at Kilmarnock, 1786. 1 vol. 8vo.
2nd edition, published at Edinburgh, 1787. 1 vol. 8vo.
3rd edition, published at London, 1787. 1 vol. 8vo.
4th edition, published at London, 1797. 2 vols. 8vo.
Letters addressed to Clarinda, Glasgow. 1802. (Suppressed.)

First collected edition of his Works published by Dr. Currie, at Liverpool. 4 vols. 8vo. 1800.

Best edition, with Life by Allan Cunningham. 8 vols. 8vo. 1834.

CAMPBELL (JOHN, LORD).

Lord High Chancellor, &c.

Born September 15, 1781. Educated at the Grammar School at Cupar, and at the University of St. Andrew's. Called to the Bar in 1806. Made Queen's Counsel in 1827. Elected M.P. for Stafford in 1830. Appointed Solicitor-General in November 1832, and Attorney-General in 1834. Elected M.P. for Edinburgh in the same year. Raised to the Peerage in 1841, and appointed Chancellor for Ireland. Made Chancellor of the Duchy of Lancaster in 1846. In 1850 appointed Chief Justice of the Court of Queen's Bench. Created Lord High Chancellor in 1859. Died June 23, 1861.

Lives of the Lord Chancellors and Keepers of the Great Seal of England, from the earliest times till the Reign of George IV. 10 vols. 8vo. 1856.

Lives of the Chief Justices of England, from the Norman Conquest till the death of Lord Tenterden. 3 vols. 8vo. 1849-57.

Shakspeare's Legal Arguments Considered. 8vo. 1859.
Speeches at the Bar and in the House of Commons, 1842.
Reports at Nisi Prius, &c.

CANNING (RIGHT HON. GEORGE, M.P.)

Department of Secretary of State, Foreign, &c.

Born April 11, 1770. Educated at Hyde Abbey School, Winchester, at Eton, and at Christ Church College, Oxford. Elected M.P. for Newport, Isle of Wight, in 1793. Appointed Under-Secretary of State for the Foreign Department in January 1796. Made Privy Councillor and Treasurer of the Navy in 1804. Again appointed Secretary of State for Foreign Affairs in March 1807: retired October 1809. In 1814 went as Minister to the Court of Lisbon. Became President of the Board of Control in 1816. In 1822 appointed for the third time Secretary of State for Foreign Affairs; and, in April 1827, First Lord of the Treasury. Died in August 1827.

Contributions to the Microcosm. 2 vols. 1793.
Originated and contributed to the Anti-Jacobin Review.
Speeches. 6 vols. 8vo. 1828–45.

CARY (REV. HENRY FRANCIS).

British Museum.

Born at Gibraltar in 1772. Educated at the Grammar Schools at Uxbridge, Rugby, and Birmingham. Admitted Commoner at Christ Church, Oxford, in 1790. Appointed Assistant Keeper of Printed Books in the British Museum in 1825. Resigned in 1832. Died August 14, 1844.

Minor Poems and Odes. 1787–88.
Translation of Dante. 8vo. 1814.
Lives of the English Poets from Johnson to Kirke White.
Edited editions of the poets Pope, Cowper, Milton Thomson, and Young.
Translations of Aristophanes and Pindar.
Various Contributions to the Gentleman's and London Magazines.

CAVENDISH (FRANCIS WILLIAM HENRY).

Department of Secretary of State, Foreign.

First employed in the Foreign Office in 1846, regularly appointed in 1848. Was Précis Writer to Lord John Russell, and also to the Earl of

Clarendon, when Secretaries of State for Foreign Affairs. Promoted to an Assistant Clerkship in 1859.

The Foreign-Office List, a Diplomatic and Consular Handbook. (Compiled in conjunction with Mr. Edward Hertslet, of the Foreign Office.) Published annually since 1842.

CHADWICK (EDWIN).

Poor Law Board and Board of Health.

Born January 24, 1801. Appointed Secretary to the Poor Law Board in 1834. Removed to the Board of Health in 1848. Retired in 1854.

Report upon the Sanitary Condition of the Labouring Population of Great Britain. 3 vols. folio and 8vo. 1842.

Report on Interment in Towns.

Contributions to the Westminster and London Reviews.

CLELAND (JAMES, LL.D.)

Superintendent of Public Works, Glasgow.

Born in 1770. Died in 1840.

Annals of Glasgow, comprising accounts of the Public Buildings, &c. &c. 2 vols. 1816.

Census and Statistics of Glasgow.
Enumeration of the Inhabitants of Glasgow.
Enumeration of the Inhabitants of Scotland.
Public Institutions of Glasgow.

COLE (HENRY, C.B.)

Record Office and Department of Science and Art.

Originally in the Record Office, now Secretary of the Department of Science and Art, and General Superintendent of the South Kensington Museum.

Holidays spent near London. 1842.
Handbook to Westminster Abbey. 1842.
Handbook to Picture Galleries. 1842.
Handbook to Hampton Court. 1843.
Handbook to National Gallery. 1843.
Handbook to Temple Church. 1843.
Handbook to Canterbury. 1843.
Day's Excursions out of London. 1843.
First Exercises in Light, Shade, and Colour. 16mo. 1846.

COLEBROOKE (HENRY THOMAS, F.R.S.)

East India Company.

Born in the year 1765. Appointed to a Writership in the service of the East India Company in 1782. Died March 18, 1837.

Twelve Views of Places in the Kingdom of Mysore, with descriptions. 1794.

Translation of the Digest of Hindu Law of Inheritance. 4 vols. 4to. 1800.

Remarks on the Husbandry and Internal Commerce of Bengal. 8vo. 1806.

Grammar of the Sanscrit Language. Folio. 1805.

Dictionary of the Sanscrit Language. 4to. 1808

Algebra and Arithmetic of the Hindus. 4to. 1817.

State of the Cape of Good Hope in 1822. 8vo. 1822.

Essays on Miscellaneous Subjects. 2 vols. 8vo. 1837.

Essays on the Religion &c. of the Hindus. 8vo. 1858.

COLMAN (GEORGE, the younger).

Lord Chamberlain's Department.

Born October 21, 1762. Educated at Westminster School, Christchurch College, Oxford, and King's College, Aberdeen. Appointed by George IV. Licenser and Examiner of Plays Died October 26, 1836.

Two to One : a play. 8vo. 1784.

The Iron Chest: a play. 8vo. 1796.

The Heir at Law: a play. 8vo.

My Nightgown and Slippers. 4to. 1797.

Broad Grins. 8vo. 1802.

Poetical Vagaries. 4to. 1812.

Vagaries Vindicated, &c. 4to. 1813.
Posthumous Letters of Celebrated Men. 4to. 1820.
Random Records. 2 vols. 8vo. 1830.
Various Plays, Prologues, Epilogues, &c. &c.

CONGLETON (HENRY PARNELL, LORD).

Department of Paymaster-General.

Born July 3, 1776. Educated at Eton and at Cambridge. Elected M.P. for Portarlington in 1802, and for Queen's County in 1806. Appointed a Lord of the Treasury in Ireland in 1806, and Secretary at War in 1831. Returned M.P. for Dundee in 1833. Was Paymaster-General and Treasurer of the Ordnance and Navy from 1835 till 1841. Created Baron Congleton in 1841. Died June 8, 1842.

Observations on the Currency of Ireland, and upon the Course of Exchange between London and Dublin. 8vo. 1804.

The Principles of Currency and Exchange, illustrated by Observations on the State of Ireland. 8vo. 1805.

An Historical Apology for the Irish Catholics. 8vo. 1807.

A History of the Penal Laws against the Irish Catholics, from the Treaty of Limerick to the Union. 8vo. 1808.

Treatise on the Corn Trade and Agriculture. 8vo. 1809.

Observations on the Irish Butter Acts. 8vo. 1825.

Observations on Paper Money, Banking, and Overtrading. 8vo. 1827.

On Financial Reform. 8vo. 1830.

A Plain Statement of the Power of the Bank of England and of the use it has made of it; with a Refutation of the Objections made to the Scotch System of Banking, &c. 8vo. 1832.

COURTNEY (JOHN, M.P.)

The Treasury.

Was Secretary to the Marquis of Townshend when Lord-Lieutenant of Ireland. Appointed a Commissioner of the Treasury in 1806. Died 1816.

Poetical Review of the Literary and Moral Character of Dr. Johnson.

Philosophical Reflections on the French Revolution.

COWPER (WILLIAM).

House of Lords.

Born at Berkhampstead, Herts, November 26, 1731. Educated for the legal profession at

Westminster School. Called to the Bar in 1754. Appointed a Commissioner in Bankruptcy in 1759. Transferred to the House of Lords as Clerk of Committees and Reading Clerk in 1763, and subsequently Clerk of the Journals. Died April 25, 1800.

Anti-Thelyphthora. 4to. 1781.
Poems. 1st edition. 1782.
John Gilpin. 24mo. 1783.
The Task. 12mo. 1784.
Poems and Translations have gone through innumerable editions.

CRAWFURD (JOHN, F.R.S.)

British Resident at Java.

History of the Indian Archipelago. 3 vols. 1820.
View of the Present State and Future Prospects of the Free Trade and Colonisation of India. 8vo. 1829.
Journal of an Embassy from the Governor-General of India to the Court of Siam and Cochin China. 2 vols. 1830.
An Enquiry into some of the Principal Monopolies of the East India Company. 8vo. 1830.
Journal of an Embassy from the Governor-General of India to the Court of Ava. 2 vols. 1834.
Chinese Monopoly Examined.
Inquiry into the System of Taxation in India. 8vo. 1839.
Malay Grammar and Dictionary. 2 vols. 8vo. 1852.

CROKER (RIGHT HON. J. WILSON).

Admiralty.

Born December 20, 1780. Educated at Trinity College, Dublin. Entered at Lincoln's Inn in 1800. Called to the Irish bar in 1802. Elected M.P. for Downpatrick in 1808. Appointed Secretary to the Admiralty in 1809. From 1809 till 1832 represented in Parliament, Downpatrick, Athlone, Yarmouth, Bodmin, and the University of Dublin. Sworn a Member of the Privy Council in 1828. Died 1857.

Familiar Epistles on the Irish Stage. 8vo. 1803.
Intercepted Letter from China. 8vo. 1805.
The State of Ireland: Past and Present. 1807.
A Letter to the Earl of Liverpool proposing to finish the East Wing of Somerset House for National Galleries. 8vo. 1823.
Edited Boswell's Life of Johnson. 4 vols. 8vo. 1831.
Edited Memoirs of the Reign of George III. by Lord Harvey.
Edited Walpole's Letters to Lord Hertford.
Essays on the Early Period of the French Revolution. 8vo. 1857.
History of the Guillotine. 12mo. 1853.
Contributed to and edited the Quarterly Review for more than 25 years.

CROKER (THOMAS CROFTON, F.S.A.)

Admiralty.

Born at Cork, January 15, 1798. Appointed to a Clerkship in the Admiralty in 1819. Retired in 1850. Died August 8, 1854.

Researches in the South of Ireland, &c. &c. 4to. 1824.
The Fairy Legends and Traditions of the South of Ireland. 1825.
Legends of the Lakes, &c. 1829.
Tour of M. Boullage Le Gonz in Ireland, 1644. 12mo. 1837.
Popular Songs of Ireland. 8vo. 1839.
Historical Songs of Ireland. 8vo. 1839. (For the Percy Society.)
Adventures of Barney Mahoney.
My Village *versus* Our Village.
Walk from London to Fulham. 8vo. 1860.
Various Antiquarian Papers in the Gentleman's Magazine, &c.

CUMBERLAND (RICHARD).

Board of Trade, &c.

Born February 19, 1732. Educated at Westminster School, and Trinity College, Cambridge.

Appointed Secretary to Lord Halifax when Viceroy of Ireland in 1760: and Secretary to the Board of Trade in 1775. Employed to conduct a secret negotiation at the Courts of Spain and Portugal in 1780. Retired from the public service in 1782. Died May 7, 1811.

Anecdotes of Eminent Painters in Spain during 16th and 17th century. 2 vols. 1782.
Descriptive Catalogue of several Paintings in the Palace at Madrid. 1787.
Arundel: a novel. 2 vols. 1789.
Calvary, or the Death of Christ: a poem. 4to. 1792.
Henry: a novel. 4 vols. 1795.
The Observer: a collection of Essays. 6 vols. 8vo. 1798.
Memoirs: written by himself. 4to. 1806.
The Exodian: a poem. 4to. 1807–8.
Retrospection: a poem. 4to. 1811.
John de Lancaster: a novel. 3 vols.
The West Indian: a comedy, 1771; and other dramatic works.

CUNNINGHAM (PETER, F.S.A.)

Audit Office.

Born April 7, 1816. Educated at Christ's Hospital. Appointed to a clerkship in the office of the Commissioners for Auditing the

Public Accounts in 1835: promoted to the Chief Clerkship in 1854. Retired from the Public Service February 4, 1859.

Edited the Works of Drummond of Hawthornden. 1 vol. 8vo. 1833.

Songs of England and Scotland. 2 vols. 8vo. 1835.

Edited 2nd edition of Campbell's Specimens of the British Poets, with additions. 8vo. 1841.

Handbook to Westminster Abbey. 12mo. 1842.

Life of Inigo Jones. 8vo. 1848.

Handbook of London, Past and Present. 2 vols. 8vo. 1849.

Modern London. 12mo. 1851.

The Story of Nell Gwyn. 8vo. 1852.

Edited the Works of Oliver Goldsmith. 4 vols. 8vo. 1854.

Edited Lives of the Poets, by Johnson, with additional Lives. 3 vols. 8vo. 1854.

Letters of Horace Walpole, chronologically arranged. 9 vols. 8vo. 1857-58.

Various contributions to the Art Journal, The Builder, The Athenæum, &c.

CURRAN (RIGHT HON. JOHN PHILPOT).

Master of the Rolls.

Born July 24, 1750. Educated at the Grammar School at Middleton, and at Trinity College, Dublin. Entered at the Middle Temple, London, in 1773. Called to the Irish Bar in 1775. Elected M.P. for Kilbeggan in the Irish Parliament 1782. Appointed Master of the Rolls in 1806. Resigned 1813. Died October 14, 1817.

Various Minor Poems.

Speeches on the late very interesting State Trials, Dublin. 8vo. 1808.

DALLAS (SIR GEORGE, BART., M.P.)

East India Company.

Born April 6, 1758. Educated at Geneva. Appointed to a Writership in the East India Company's service in 1776. Returned to England in 1785. Created a Baronet in 1798. Represented Newport, Isle of Wight, in Parliament for some time. Died January, 1833.

A Pamphlet, attributing the British Supremacy in India to Warren Hastings. 8vo. 1789.

The Indian Guide: a poem.

Thoughts, &c., with Remarks upon the Policy of a War with France. 1793.

Various Treatises on the East India Trade and Policy.

Biographical Memoir of Captain Sir Peter Parker.

Various political works relative to the State of Ireland.

DALRYMPLE (ALEXANDER).

Admiralty and East India Company.

Born July 24, 1737. Appointed to a Writership in the East India Company's service in 1753. Became Member of Council at Madras in 1775: recalled in 1777. Appointed Hydrographer to the East India Company in 1779, and Hydrographer to the Admiralty in 1795; retained the office till May, 1808. Died June 19, 1808.

An Account of the Discoveries made in the South Pacific previous to 1764. 8vo. 1767.

Plan for Extending the Commerce of this Kingdom and the East India Company. 8vo. 1769.

Collection of Voyages &c. in the South Pacific. 2 vols. 4to. 1769–71.

Collection of Voyages chiefly in the Southern Atlantic Ocean. 4to. 1775.

Collection of Plans of Ports in the East Indies. 4to. 1775.

The Oriental Repertory. 2 vols. 4to. 1791–1808.

Collection of English Songs, with an Appendix of Original Pieces. 8vo. 1796.

Various works of minor importance.

DALRYMPLE (SIR JOHN, BART.)

Exchequer, Scotland.

Born in 1726. Appointed Baron of Exchequer in Scotland in 1776. Retired in 1807, Died in 1810.

An Essay towards a General History of Feudal Property in Great Britain. 8vo. 1757.

Considerations on the Polity of Entails in a Nation. 8vo. 1765.

Memoirs of Great Britain and Ireland. 3 vols. 4to. 1771.

The Question Considered whether Wool should be allowed to be Exported when the price is low at Home, on paying a Duty to the Public. 8vo. 1781.

DEAN (R. B.)

Chairman of the Board of Customs.

Remarks on the Revenue of Customs, with a few observations on a late work of Sir H. Parnell, on Financial Reform. 8vo. 1830.

DE LA BECHE (SIR H. T.)

Museum of Geology.

Born in the year 1796. Educated at the School of Ottery St. Mary, and at the Royal Military

College, Great Marlow (now Sandhurst). Served for a short time in the army. Appointed Director of the Geological Survey, and of the Museum of Practical Geology and School of Mines in 1835. Knighted in 1848. Died April 13, 1855.

Manual of Geology. 8vo. 1831.
Researches in Theoretical Geology. 8vo. 1834.
How to observe—Geology. 8vo. 1835.
Report of the Geology of Cornwall. 8vo. 1839.
Geological Observer. 8vo. 1853.
Geological Notes.
Sections and Views of Geological Phenomena.
Geological Report, Devon and Cornwall.
Various contributions to the Transactions of the Geological Society, &c.

DERBY (EDWARD GEOFFREY SMITH STANLEY, RIGHT HON. EARL OF, K.G.)

S. S. Colonial. The Treasury.

Born March 29, 1799. Educated at Christ Church, Oxford. Obtained the Latin Verse Prize in 1819. Elected M.P. for Stockbridge in 1822; for Preston in 1826; for Windsor in 1830; and for North Lancashire in 1832. Summoned to the House of Peers in 1844. Appointed Under-Secretary of State for the Colonies in 1828. Was Chief Secretary for Ireland from 1830 till March 1833. Secretary of State for the Colonies from March 1833 till July 1834; and from September 1841 till December 1845. Prime Minister and First Lord of the Treasury from February to December 1852; and from February 1858 to June 1859. Elected Lord Rector of Glasgow University in 1834, and Chancellor of the University of Oxford in October 1852.

The Iliad of Homer rendered into English blank verse. 2 vols. 8vo. 1864.

DILKE (CHARLES WENTWORTH).

Navy Pay-Office.

Born December 8, 1789. Held an appointment in the Navy Pay Office till the abolition of the office in 1836, when he received a retired allowance, and became proprietor and editor of the 'Athenæum' weekly newspaper, which he conducted till 1846. Was editor of the 'Daily

News' for a short time in 1846. Died August 10, 1864.

A Collection of Old English Plays. 6 vols. 8vo. 1814.
Edited the Athenæum from 1836 till 1846.
Edited the Daily News in 1846.
Various contributions to the Reviews and Magazines.

DISRAELI (RIGHT HON. B., M.P.)

Chancellor of the Exchequer.

Born December 1805. Educated at Winchester School. Elected M.P. for Maidstone in 1837; for Shrewsbury in 1841; and for Buckinghamshire in 1847. Appointed Chancellor of the Exchequer in March 1852. Retired in December of the same year. Again appointed in March 1858. Resigned in June 1859.

Vivian Grey. 8vo. 1827.
Voyage of Captain Papanilla. 8vo. 1828.
The Young Duke. 8vo. 1831.
The Wondrous Tale of Alroy. 8vo. 1833.
Revolutionary Epic. Parts 1 and 2. 4to. 1834.
The Crisis Examined. 8vo. 1834.
A Vindication of the English Constitution. 1835.

Letters of Runnymede. 8vo. 1836.
Henrietta Temple: a novel. 8vo. 1837.
Venetia. 8vo. 1837.
Count Alarcos: a tragedy. 8vo. 1838.
Coningsby: a novel. 8vo. 1844.
Contarini Fleming. 8vo. 1846.
Ixion in Heaven. 8vo. 1847.
Sybil. 8vo. 1845.
Tancred, or the New Crusade. 8vo. 1847.
Life and Character of Charles I., by Isaac Disraeli. Edited by B. Disraeli. 1850.
Biography of Lord George Bentinck. 8vo. 1851.
England and France.
Various Political Pamphlets.

DOVER (G. J. AGAR ELLIS) LORD.

Woods and Forests.

Born January 14, 1797. Educated at Christ Church College, Oxford. Elected M.P. for Heytesbury in 1818. Appointed Chief Commissioner of Woods and Forests in 1830. Died July 10, 1833.

Catalogue of the Principal Pictures in Flanders and Holland, 1822. 8vo. 1826. (Privately printed).
True History of the Iron Mask, extracted from Documents in the French Archives. 8vo. 1826.

Historical Inquiries respecting the Character of Edward Hyde, Earl of Clarendon. 8vo. 1827.

The Ellis Correspondence. 2 vols. 8vo. 1828.

Life of Frederick the Great. 2 vols. 8vo. 1832.

Edited Letters of Sir Horace Walpole to Sir Horace Mann.

Various Contributions to the Quarterly and Edinburgh Reviews, &c.

DRUMMOND (RIGHT HON. SIR WILLIAM, F.R.S. M.P.)

Department of Secretary of State, Foreign.

Appointed Envoy Extraordinary to the King of the Two Sicilies in 1801. Ambassador to Turkey in 1803, and again Envoy Extraordinary to the two Sicilies in 1806. Died at Rome in March, 1828.

A Review of the Government of Sparta and Athens. 8vo. 1794.

A Metrical Translation of the Satires of Persius. 8vo. 1798.

Academical Questions. 4to. 1805.

Herculanensia, or Archæological and Philological Dissertations, MSS. found at Herculaneum. 4to. 1810.

The Ædipus Judaicus. 8vo. 1811.

Essay on a Punic Inscription found in the Island of Malta. 4to. 1811.

Odin: a poem. 4to. 1817.

Remarks on the Origin of several Empires, States, and Cities. 4 vols. 8vo. 1828.

Memoir on the Antiquity of the Zodiacs of Enoch and Dendersh. 8vo. 1828.

ELLIS (SIR HENRY, KNIGHT).

British Museum.

Born in the year 1777. Educated at Merchant Taylor's School, and St. John's College, Oxford. Appointed Sub-Librarian of the Bodleian Library in 1827; and Principal Librarian of the British Museum in the same year. Resigned in 1856.

History and Antiquities of the Parish of St. Leonard, Shoreditch, &c. 4to. 1798.

Edited Brande's Popular Antiquities. 2 vols. 4to. 1813.

Original Letters, illustrative of English History, including numerous Royal Letters from Autographs in the British Museum :—

1st Series, 3 vols. 1824.
2nd Series, 4 vols. 1827.
3rd Series, 4 vols. 1846.

Edited Blair's Chronological Tables. Imperial 8vo. 1851.

An Introduction to the Doomsday Survey.

An Introduction to Dugdale's Monasticon.

Various Contributions to the Archæologia, &c., &c.

FARR (William., M.D., F.R.S.)

General Register Office.

Born November 30, 1807. Educated at the London University, and at the University at Paris. Received an appointment in the office of the Registrar-General in 1838; is now Superintendent of the Statistical Department of the Registrar-General of Births, Deaths, and Marriages.

Edited the British Annals of Medicine. 1837.

Editor of the Quarterly Returns of Births, Deaths, and Marriages.

Editor of the Tables of Mortality.

Various Reports on Public Health: Income Tax and Finance connected with Life Assurance.

Contributed the Article 'Vital Statistics' in McCulloch's Statistics of the British Empire.

FONBLANQUE (Albany W.)

Board of Trade.

England under Seven Administrations. 3 vols. 8vo. 1837.

Edited the Examiner Newspaper for many years.

FORBES (EDWARD, F.R.S.)

Museum of Practical Geology.

Born in the Isle of Man, February 12, 1815. Educated at the Edinburgh University. Appointed Professor of Zoology and Palæontology to the Government School of Mines in 1846. Died November 17, 1854.

History of British Star Fishes. 8vo. 1840–41.
History of British Mollusca and their Shells. 4 vols. 1853.
Travels in Lycia Syria.
Geological and Palæontological Map of the British Isles.
Map of the Distribution of Marine Life.
Natural History of the European Seas. 12mo. 1859.
Synopsis of British Naked-Eyed Pulmograde Medusæ. 4to.
Tertiary Fluvio Marine Formation of the Isle of Wight. Royal 8vo. 1856.
Various Scientific Papers in different journals of Science.

FORSHALL (REV. JOSIAH, M.A., F.R.S.)

British Museum.

Born in 1796. Educated at Exeter College, Oxford. Appointed Assistant-Keeper of the

Manuscripts in the British Museum in 1824; became Keeper in 1828, and Secretary in 1837. For 34 years Chaplain to the Foundling Hospital. Died December 18, 1863.

- The Holy Bible, from the Latin Vulgate of Wycliffe. 4 vols. 4to. Edited by Rev. J. Forshall and Sir F. Madden.
- The Gospels of St. Mark, St. Luke, and St. John, with Chronological References. 12mo. 1861.
- Letter to the Archbishop of Canterbury on Church Reform. 8vo. 1833.
- Catalogue of the MSS. in the British Museum. 3 parts. Folio. 1834–40.
- Description of Greek Papyri in the British Museum. Part I. 4to. 1839.
- Remonstrance of 1395 against Romish Corruptions in the Church. 12mo. 1853.
- Various Sermons.

FORSTER (JOHN).

Commissioner in Lunacy.

Born in 1812. Educated at the London University. Is a Member of the Inner Temple. Appointed Secretary to the Commissioners in Lunacy in 1856; is now one of the Commissioners.

Lives of the Statesmen of the Commonwealth. 7 vols. 8vo. 1840.
Judgment of Brutus: a tragedy. 8vo. 1843.
Life of Oliver Goldsmith. 2nd edition. 1854.
Defoe and Churchill. 16mo. 1855.
Historical and Biographical Essays. 2 vols. 1858.
Debates on the Grand Remonstrance, November and December 1641. 8vo. 1860.
Arrest of the Five Members by Charles I. 8vo. 1860.
Edited the Examiner Newspaper from 1847 to 1858.

FOX (RIGHT HON. CHARLES JAMES, M.P.)

Admiralty, the Treasury, and Secretary of State's Office, Foreign Department.

Born February 24, 1749. Educated at Westminster School, at Eton and at Oxford. Elected M.P. for Midhurst in 1768. Appointed a Lord of the Admiralty in 1770, and a Lord of the Treasury in 1773; became Secretary of State for the Foreign Department in 1782, and again in April 1783; resigned in December; resumed the office on the death of Mr. Pitt, in January 1806. Died on September 13, 1806.

History of the Early Part of the Reign of James II. 4to. 1808.
Speeches in Parliament. 6 vols. 8vo. 1815. With Biographical and Critical Introduction, by Lord Erskine.

FRANCIS (SIR PHILIP, M.P.)

Foreign Office, War Department and East India Company.

Born in Dublin October 22, 1740. Educated at St. Paul's School, London. Appointed to a Clerkship in the Foreign Office in 1757; was Secretary to the Embassy to Portugal in 1760. Transferred from the Foreign Department to the War Office in 1763; retired in 1772. Nominated a Member of Council of Bengal, East India Company's Service, in 1773; resigned in 1780. Elected M.P. for Yarmouth, Isle of Wight, in 1784, and for Appleby in 1802. Created K.C.B. October 29, 1806. Retired from Parliament in 1807. Died December 22, 1818.

Attributed Author of the 'Letters of Junius.'
Political Pamphlets, &c. (26 in number.)
Speeches in Parliament.

GELL (SIR WILLIAM).

Foreign Office and Lord Chamberlain's Department.

Born in 1777. Educated at Jesus College, and was for some time a Fellow of Emanuel College, Cambridge. Appointed Special Commissioner to the Ionian Islands in 1803, received an appointment in the Lord Chamberlain's Department in 1814. Died February 4, 1836.

The Topography of Troy and its Vicinity. Folio. 1804.
The Geography and Antiquities of Ithaca. 4to. 1807.
Itinerary of Greece. 4to. 1810.
Pompeiana, or Observations upon the Topography, &c. of Pompeii. 1st and 2nd Series. Imp. 8vo. 1817-19.
Itinerary of Morea. 8vo. 1817.
Narrative of a Journey in the Morea. 8vo. 1823.
Topography of Rome and its Vicinity. 2 vols. 8vo. 1834 and 1846.
The Topography, Edifices, and Ornaments of Pompeii: the Result of Excavations since 1819. 2 vols. 8vo. 1832.

GIFFORD (WILLIAM).

Lord Chamberlain's Department.

Born in April 1757. Educated at Exeter College, Oxford. Edited in 1797 the Anti-Jacobin, a weekly paper started under the auspices of Canning and Pitt. Edited the Quarterly Review from its commencement in 1809 till 1824; held the appointment of Paymaster of the Gentlemen Pensioners in the Office of the Lord Chamberlain, and was Comptroller of the Lottery. Died December 31, 1826.

The Baviad: a satire. 1st edit. 4to. 1791. 6th edit. 1800.
The Mæviad: a satire. 1st edit. 4to. 1794. 6th edit. 1800.
Edited the Anti-Jacobin from 1797 till 1798.
Translation of Juvenal and Persius. 1802.
Edited Massinger's Plays. 4 vols. 8vo. 1805.
„ Ben Jonson's Works. 9 vols. 8vo. 1816.
„ Ford's Works. 2 vols. 1827.
„ Shirley's Works. 6 vols. 8vo. 1833.
Various Poetical Satires, including 'Epistle to Peter Pindar.'
Edited the Quarterly Review from 1809 to 1824.

GLADSTONE (RIGHT HON. WM. EWART, M.P.)

Chancellor of the Exchequer.
The Treasury, Colonial Department, Board of Trade, Mint.

Born December 29, 1809. Educated at Eton and Christ Church College, Oxford. Elected M.P. for Newark in 1832. Appointed a Lord of the Treasury in 1834, and Under-Secretary for the Colonies in 1835; retired in April, 1836; was Vice-President of the Board of Trade from 1841 to 1843; and President of the Board of

Trade and Master of the Mint from May 1843 till 1845; was Secretary of State for the Colonies from 1845 to July 1846. Elected M.P. for the University of Oxford in 1847. Appointed Chancellor of the Exchequer in December 1852; resigned in February 1855. Again appointed in June 1859.

The State in its Relations with the Church. 8vo. 1838.
Church Principles considered in their Results. 8vo. 1840.
Letters to the Earl of Aberdeen on the State Prosecution of the Neapolitan Government.
Remarks on Recent Commercial Legislation. 8vo. 1845.
Selections from the Liturgy for Family Use. 1845.
Studies on Homer and the Homeric Age. 3 vols. 8vo. 1858.
Various Contributions to the Quarterly Review, &c.
Translated Farini's History of Roman States, 1815–50. 4 vols. 8vo. 1851–54.
Speeches, &c.

GLEIG (THE REV. G. R.)

War Department.

Born April 20, 1796. Educated at the University of Glasgow and at Balliol College, Oxford. Served in the Army from 1812. Appointed

Chaplain to Chelsea Hospital in 1834. Chaplain-General of the Forces in 1844; and Inspector-General of Military Schools in 1846.

Allan Breck. 3 vols. 8vo. 1844.
British Army at Washington. 8vo. 1847.
Chelsea Hospital. 3 vols. 8vo. 1838.
Chelsea Pensioners. 3 vols. 8vo. 1829.
Chronicles of Waltham. 3 vols. 1835.
Country Curate. 2 vols. 1834.
Family History of England. 3 vols. 1835.
Germany, Hungary, &c., visited in 1837. 3 vols. 1839.
Guide to the Sacrament of the Lord's Supper. 12mo. 1835.
History of British India. 4 vols. 18mo. 1831.
History of England abridged for Schools. 12mo. 1850.
History of the Bible. 2 vols. 12mo. 1845.
The Hussar. 2 vols. 1837.
Katherine Randolph. 12mo. 1857.
Leipsic Campaign. 12mo. 1852.
Life of Arthur Duke of Wellington. 8vo. 1862.
Life of Lord Clive. 12mo. 1848.
Light Dragoon. 2 vols. 1844.
Lives of British Military Commanders. 3 vols. 1831.
Memoirs of Warren Hastings. 3 vols. 1841.
Sale's Brigade in Affghanistan. 8vo. 1846.
Sketch of the Military History of Great Britain. 1845.
Story of the Battle of Waterloo. 8vo. 1847.
The Subaltern. 1825.
Traditions of Chelsea College. 3 vols. 1838.
Veterans of Chelsea Hospital. 3 vols. 1843.
Elementary School Series, &c. &c.

GRAHAM (Thomas).

The Royal Mint.

Born in December 1805. Educated at the Grammar School at Glasgow, and at the Universities of Glasgow and Edinburgh. Originally appointed to the Mint as Assayer. On the retirement of Sir John Herschel from the Mastership of the Mint in 1855, received the appointment of Master.

Elements of Chemistry. 1842.
Various Contributions to the Transactions of the Royal Society.

GRANT (Charles, M.P.)

East India Company.

Born in the year 1746. Appointed to a Writership at Bengal, East India Company's service, in 1772, and Secretary to the Board of Trade. On returning to England in 1790, became a Director of the East India Company. Elected M.P. for Inverness in 1802. Appointed Deputy-Chairman of the India Company in 1804, and Chairman in 1805. Died 1822.

Observations on the State of Society among the Asiatic Subjects of Great Britain. 1797.

GODWIN (WILLIAM).

Exchequer Office.

Born at Wisbeach March 3, 1756. Educated at the Dissenter's College at Hoxton. Officiated as a Dissenting Minister till 1783; became Editor of the Annual Register in 1784. Appointed Yeoman Usher of the Exchequer in 1832. Died April 7, 1836.

Sketches of History: a series of Six Sermons. 12mo. 1784.

An Enquiry concerning Political Justice and its Influence on General Virtue and Happiness. 2 vols. 4to. 1793.

Caleb Williams: a tale. 3 vols. 8vo. 1794.

Enquirer, Reflections on Education, Manners, and Literature. 8vo. 1797.

St. Leon: a tale. 4 vols. 8vo. 1799.

History of Life and Age of Geoffry Chaucer, &c. 2 vols. 4to. 1803.

Fleetwood: a tale. 3 vols. 1805.

Antonio: a tragedy. 8vo. 1800.

Faulkner: a tragedy. 8vo. 1808.

An Essay on Sepulchres, &c. 12mo. 1809.

Lives of E. and J. Philips, Nephews of Milton, including Particulars of the Political and Literary History of their times. 4to. 1815.

Mandeville: a tale. 3 vols. 1817.

Inquiry on Increase of Population. 8vo. 1820.
History of the Commonwealth of England, &c. 4 vols. 8vo. 1824.
Cloudesley: a novel. 3 vols. 8vo. 1830.
Deloraine: a novel. 8vo. 1833.
Lives of the Necromancers. 8vo. 1834.
History of the Gods of Greece and Rome.
History of England.
Outlines of English History.
History of Greece.
History of Rome.
Outlines of English Grammar.
Fables, Ancient and Modern.
Conducted the Annual Register from 1784.

GRATTAN (THOMAS COLLEY).

Department of Secretary of State, Foreign.

Born in Dublin, 1796. Served as a Volunteer in the South American Army against Spain. Appointed Gentleman of the Privy Chamber to William IV. in 1831, and British Consul at Boston, United States, in 1839: retired in favour of his son in 1848. Died July 1864.

Phillibert: a poetical romance. 8vo. 1819.
Highways and Byways. 1st, 2nd, and 3rd series, 8vo. 1823.

Ben Nazir, the Saracen: a play. 8vo. 1824.
Tales of Men and Cities. 8vo. 1829.
Tracts of Travel. 8vo. 1831.
History of the Netherlands. 8vo. 1831.
Heiress of Bruges. 8vo. 1831.
Jacqueline of Holland. 8vo. 1831.
Master Passion. 8vo. 1845.
Cagot's Hut. 8vo. 1847.
Agnes de Mansfeldt. 8vo. 1849.
Woman of Colour. 8vo. 1847.
Curse of the White Lady, &c. 1857.
England and the Disrupted States of America. 1861.
Beaten Paths and Those who Trod them. 1862.
Legends of the Rhine.
The Boundary Question in America: a pamphlet.

GRAY (GEORGE R.)

British Museum, Department of Zoology.

Genera of Birds, by G. R. Gray and D. M. Mitchell. 3 vols. imp. 4to. 1837–49.

GREG (WILLIAM RATHBONE).

Customs and H.M. Stationery Office.

Son of Samuel Greg of Manchester, and brother of Robert Hyde Greg of Norcliffe Hall, County of Chester, and Coles Park, Hertfordshire, formerly M.P. for Manchester. Appointed a Commissioner of Customs in 1856; transferred to the Comptrollership of H.M. Stationery Office in December 1864.

The Creed of Christendom ; its Foundations and Superstructure. 8vo. 1851.

Investments for the Working Classes. 12mo. 1852.

Essays on Political and Social Science. 2 vols. 8vo. 1853. (Contributions the Edinburgh Review.)

GRENVILLE (RIGHT HON. WILLIAM WYNDHAM, LORD).

Home Office, Foreign Office, Paymaster-General's Office, and the Treasury.

Born in 1759. Educated at Eton, and at the University of Oxford. Appointed Secretary to Earl Temple in 1782, when Lord-Lieutenant in Ireland. Elected M.P. for Buckinghamshire in 1782. Made Paymaster-General of the Army 1783. Elected Speaker of the House of Commons in 1789; became Secretary of State for the Home Department in the same year. Raised to the Peerage in 1790. In June 1791, appointed Secretary of State for the Foreign Department; retained the office till 1801. On the death of Mr. Pitt, in 1806, became Premier and First Lord of the Treasury. Elected Chancellor of the University of Oxford in 1809. Died January 12, 1834.

Edited Letters of Lord Chatham to his Nephew. 8vo. 1804.

A New Plan of Finance. 8vo. 1806.

Nugæ Metricæ. Royal 4to. 1824. (Privately printed.)

Oxford and Lock: Defence of the University against Dugald Stewart, relative to the Expulsion of Lock from the University. 8vo. 1829.

GREY (SIR GEORGE).

S. S. Colonial Department.

Governor of South Australia and New Zealand, from December 1846, to July 1854; of the Cape of Good Hope, from 1854 till 1861. Transferred to New Zealand in 1861.

Journals of Discovery in Australia 1837, 1838, and 1839 2 vols. 8vo. 1841.

Vocabulary of the Dialect of South-West Australia. 18mo. 1841.

Polynesian Mythology and Traditions of New Zealand. 8vo. 1853.

Proverbial Sayings of the Ancestors of the New Zealand Race. 8vo. 1858.

GREY (RIGHT HON. HENRY GREY, EARL).

S. S. Colonial, S. S. Home, War Department.

Born in 1802. Educated at Trinity College, Cambridge. Elected M.P. for Winchester in 1826, for Northumberland in 1831, and for Sunderland in 1841; was Under Secretary of State for the Colonies from 1830 to 1833; for the Home Department from January to July 1834; Secretary of War from April 1835 to September 1839; and Secretary of State for the Colonies from July 1846 to February 1852.

Colonial Policy of Lord John Russell's Administration. 2 vols. 8vo. 1853.

Essay on Parliamentary Government as to Reform. 8vo. 1852.

HALHEAD (NATHANIEL BRASSEY, M.P.)

East India Company.

Born in 1751. Died in 1830.

A Code of Gentor Laws on Ordinations of the Pundits, from a Persian translation. 4to. 1776.

A Grammar of the Bengal Language. 4to. 1778.

A Narrative of the Events which have happened in Bombay and Bengal, relative to the Mahratta Empire, since July 1777.

HAMILTON (WILLIAM GERARD, M.P.)

Board of Trade, and the Exchequer Office in Ireland.

Born January 28, 1729. Educated at Winchester School, and at Oriel College, Oxford. Elected M.P. for Petersfield in 1754. Appointed Commissioner of the Board of Trade in April 1756; was Secretary to Lord Halifax when Lord-Lieutenant of Ireland, in 1761: created Irish Chancellor of the Exchequer in 1763; resigned in 1784. Died July 16, 1796.

Poems. 4to. 1750.

Parliamentary Logic.

Parliamentary Speeches, &c., with Appendix, 'Considerations on the Corn Laws, by Samuel Johnson.' 8vo. 1808.

HAMILTON (RIGHT HON. SIR WILLIAM, BART., M.P.)

Secretary of State, Foreign Department.

Born in 1730. Educated at private schools. Represented Midhurst in Parliament. Appointed

Ambassador to the Court of Naples in 1764; created K.C.B. in 1772, and a Privy Counsellor in 1791. Died April 6, 1803.

Observations on Mount Vesuvius, Mount Etna, &c.
Campi Phlegræi, Observations on the Volcanoes of the Two Sicilies. 2 vols. folio. 1776. Supplement, 1779.
Various Contributions to the Philosophical Transactions and the Archæologia.

HARDY (THOMAS D.)

Public Record Department.

Catalogue of Lord Chancellors. Royal 8vo. 1843.
Materials Relating to the History of Great Britain. Royal 8vo. parts 1 and 2. 1862.
Shakesperian Controversy. 8vo. 1862.

HASTINGS (RIGHT. HON. WARREN).

East India Company.

Born December 6, 1732. Educated at Westminster School. Appointed to a Clerkship in the India Company's service in 1750; became Member of Council at Calcutta in 1761; returned to England in 1764; resumed his duties in India in 1769; was Member of Council at Madras from that date till 1772, when he was appointed President of the Supreme Council of Bengal, and Governor-General in 1774; resigned and returned to Europe in 1785. Impeached in 1786. Trial in Westminster Hall commenced February 13, 1788; terminated on April 17, 1795, with an acquittal on every charge; took no part in public life after the trial; was created a Privy Councillor in 1818, and died on 22nd August in the same year.

A Narrative of the Insurrection at Benares in 1781. 4to. 1782.
Memoirs Relative to the State of India.
Fugitive Poetry, &c.

HATSELL (JOHN).

House of Commons.

Born in the year 1742. Educated at Queen's College, Cambridge. A Member of the Middle Temple. Appointed Chief Clerk to the House of Commons in 1768; retired in 1797. Died October 15, 1820.

A Collection of Cases of Privilege of Parliament.
Precedents of Proceedings in the House of Commons. 4to. 1781. 4th edition, 4 vols. 4to. 1818.
Rules and Standing Orders of the House of Commons.

HAWKINS (EDWARD).

British Museum.

Description of the Silver Coins of England. 8vo. 1841.

HAY (SIR JOHN H. DRUMMOND, K.C.B.)

Department of Secretary of State, Foreign.

Appointed Attaché to the Turkish Embassy in 1840, Consul General at Morocco in 1845, and Charge d'Affaires in 1847. Employed on various missions to Morocco in the years 1854, 1855, and 1856. Created a C.B. in 1857, and K.C.B. and Minister Resident to the Emperor of Morocco in 1860.

Morocco and the Moors. 12mo. 1844.
Western Barbary, its Wild Tribes and Animals.

HERTSLET (EDWARD, F.G.S.)

Department of Secretary of State, Foreign.

First employed in the Librarian's Department, Foreign Office, in 1840; became Supernumerary Clerk in 1842, and permanently appointed in 1844; became Sub-Librarian in 1855, and Librarian and Keeper of the Papers in 1857.

The Foreign Office List, a Diplomatic and Consular Handbook. (Compiled in conjunction with Mr. F. W. H. Cavendish, of the Foreign Office.) First published in 1842, and continued annually.

HERTSLET (LEWIS).

Department of Secretary of State, Foreign.

Appointed Sub-Librarian in the Foreign Office 1801; was Librarian and Keeper of the Papers from 1810 till November 1857.

A Complete Collection of the Treaties and Conventions and Reciprocal Regulations at present subsisting between Great Britain and Foreign Powers. 10 vols. 8vo. 1847-59.

HEWITT (JOHN).

War Department.

Ancient Armour and Weapons in Europe: from the Iron Period of the Northern Nations to the end of the 17th century. 3 vols. Medm. 8vo. 1855-60.

Guide to the Tower Armories and Antiquities, with Illustrations. 12mo. Various editions.

Ditto, in French. 12mo. Eleven editions.

Official Catalogue of the Tower Armories. 12mo. Published by authority of the War Office.

Contributions to the Archæological Journal, Gentleman's, Metropolitan, and New Monthly Magazines, and other serials.

HILL (SIR ROWLAND).

General Post Office.

(*Originated and Organised the Penny Postage System.*)

Born in the year 1795. Appointed Secretary to the Postmaster-General in 1846, and Secretary to the General Post Office in 1854; retired in 1864.

Post Office Reform, its Importance and Practicability. 8vo. 1837.

State and Prospects of the Penny Postage. 8vo. 1844.

HOLLAND (HENRY RICHARD VASSAL, LORD).

Privy Seal Office and Office of Duchy of Lancaster.

Born November 21, 1773. Educated at Eton and at Christchurch College, Oxford. Appointed Lord Privy Seal in 1806, and Chancellor of the Duchy of Lancaster in November 1830; retained the office, with little intermission, till 1840. Died October 22, 1840.

Lives of Lope de Vega and de Castro. 1 vol. 8vo. 1806. 2nd edition, 2 vols. 8vo. 1817.

Comedies from the Spanish. 8vo. 1807.

Edited the History of the Reign of James II., by C. J. Fox. 8vo. 1808.

A Letter to Dr. Shuttleworth in Favour of the Catholic Claims. 8vo. 1827.

Foreign Reminiscences. 8vo. 1850. (Edited by his Son.)

Memoirs of the Whig Party. 2 vols. 8vo. 1852-54.

HOLT (FRANCIS LUDLOW).

Duchy of Lancaster.

Died in September, 1844.

Treatise on Law of Bankruptcy.
„ on Law of Libel.
„ on Law of Shipping.
Reports Nisi Prius. 1815-17.
Some Dramatic Pieces.
Edited Bell's Weekly Messenger.

HOLWELL (JOHN ZEPHANIAH).

East India Company.

Born in September 1711. Educated in Holland for the Medical Profession; was Surgeon in the East India Company's Service from 1732 till 1740. Elected a Member of Council at Calcutta in 1756. Appointed Governor of Bengal in 1760; superseded at the end of the year. Died in 1798.

Narrative of Confinement in the Black Hole at Calcutta in 1758.
Indian Tracts. 8vo. 1764.
Historical Events Relating to Bengal and Indostan, &c. in 3 parts. 1765-67-71.
Various Papers on Indian Affairs. 8vo. 1774.

HOME (JOHN).

Born in the year 1722. Educated for the Church, at the Grammar School of Leith, and at the Edinburgh University; obtained a license to preach in April 1745; resigned his living in June 1757. Appointed immediately after his resignation, by Lord Bute, to the sinecure office of Conservator of Scots privileges at Campvere, with a pension of 300*l.* per annum in addition to the salary of his sinecure office. Died in 1808.

Douglas: a tragedy. 12mo. 1760.
Fatal Discovery: a tragedy.
Alonzo: a tragedy.
Alfred: a tragedy.
History of the Rebellion of 1845–6. 4to. 1802.

HOOK (THEODORE EDWARD, F.S.A.)

Department of Secretary of State, Colonial.

Born September 22, 1788. Educated at Harrow School. Appointed in 1812 Accountant-General and Treasurer to the Mauritius; recalled in January 1818. Became Editor of the 'John Bull' newspaper in 1820, and Edited the 'New Monthly Magazine' from 1836 till 1841. Died August 24, 1841.

Man of Sorrow. 3 vols. 8vo. 1809.
Sayings and Doings. 1st, 2nd and 3rd series. 1824-5-8.
Percy Mallory. 3 vols. 8vo. 1824.
Memoirs of Michael Kelly, the Composer. 2 vols. 1826.
Maxwell. 3 vols. 8vo. 1830.
Memoirs of Sir David Baird. 2 vols. 1832.
Love and Pride. 3 vols. 8vo. 1833.
The Parson's Daughter. 3 vols. 8vo. 1835.
Gilbert Gurney. 3 vols. 8vo. 1835.
Jack Brag. 3 vols. 8vo. 1837.
Pascal Bruno. 1 vol. 8vo. 1837.
Gurney Married. 3 vols. 8vo. 1839.
Births, Deaths, and Marriages. 3 vols. 8vo. 1839.
Precept and Practice. 3 vols. 1840.
Cousin Geoffrey. 3 vols. 1840.
Fathers and Sons. 3 vols. 1840.
Peregrine Bunce. 3 vols. 1842.
Widow and Marquis. 3 vols.
13 Dramatic Pieces.
Edited the John Bull Newspaper from 1820 till 1841.
Edited the New Monthly Magazine from 1836 till 1841.

HOOKER (Sir William J., D.C.L.)

Woods and Forests.

Born in the year 1785. Appointed Director of the Royal Gardens at Kew in 1841.

Exotic Flora. 3 vols. imp. 8vo. 1823-27.

Icones Filicum, Figures of Ferns. 2 vols. folio. 1829-31.

The British Flora. 1830.

Icones Plantarum, New and Rare Plants. 10 vols. 1837-54.

Baner's Genera of Ferns. Imp. 8vo. 1840.

Journal of Botany. 9 vols. 8vo. 1842-49.

Figures of Exotic Ferns. Royal 4to. 1859.

Various valuable Works on Botany, the above being the most important.

HOOLE (JOHN).

East India Company.

Born in the year 1727. Appointed to a Clerkship in the Accountant's Department, East India Company in 1741; retired in 1783. Died August 2, 1803.

Translation of Tasso. 1763.

" of Ariosto.

" of Metastasio.

Cyrus: a tragedy. 8vo. 1768.

Tymanthes: a tragedy. 8vo. 1770.

Cleonice: a tragedy. 8vo. 1775.

HORNER (LEONARD, F.R.S.)

Factory Inspector's Office.

Born in the year 1785. Educated in Edinburgh. Appointed Warden to the London University in 1827, and Inspector of Factories in 1833. Died March 5, 1864.

Memoir and Correspondence of Francis Horner. 2 vols. 8vo.

Reports &c. connected with Factories and Factory Workers.

Various Papers relative to the Mineral Kingdom.

HUME (JAMES DEACON).

The Customs and Board of Trade.

Born April 28, 1774. Educated at Westminster School. Appointed to a Clerkship in the Customs in 1790. Employed by Government in the years 1821-24 to Consolidate and Codify the Customs Statutes, resulting in the 11 Acts of Parliament passed in 1825. Transferred from the Customs to the Board of Trade, as Joint Secretary, in 1828; retired in 1840, with a pension specially granted by the Treasury, of 1,500*l.* per annum. Died January 12, 1842.

Laws of the Customs. 8vo. 1825.
Letters on the Corn Laws and on the Rights of the Working Classes. 8vo. 1834.
Various Contributions to the British and Foreign Review.
Letters in the Morning Chronicle, under the signature H. B. T.

HUNT (ROBERT).

Museum of Practical Geology.

Born September 6, 1807. Keeper of Mining Records, School of Mines.

Panthea; the Spirit of Nature. 8vo.
Practice of Photography. 8vo. 1841.
Researches in Light, &c. 8vo. 1844.
Poetry of Science; Studies of Physical Phenomena. 8vo. 1849.
Elementary Physics; Introduction to Natural Philosophy. 8vo. 1851.
Manual of Photography. 8vo. 1857.

HUSKISSON (RIGHT HON. WILLIAM, M.P.)

Alien Office, War and Colonial Department, Woods and Forests, Board of Trade and Treasury.

Born March 11, 1770. First officially employed as Secretary to Lord Gower, Ambassador at Paris, in 1790. Appointed to the Alien Office in 1793, as head of the department for the investigation of claims of French Emigrants; became Under-Secretary of State for War and the Colonies in 1795. Elected M.P. for Morpeth in 1796; was Secretary to the Treasury in 1804; retired on the death of Mr. Pitt; was again appointed in 1807, and resigned in 1809. Appointed Chief Commissioner of Woods and Forests, 1814. Elected M.P. for Liverpool in 1823. Appointed in the same year to the office of President of the Board of Trade. In 1827, on the death of Mr. Canning, nominated Secretary of State for the Colonies; retired in 1829. Died September 15, 1830, in consequence of injuries received at the opening of the Liverpool and Manchester Railway.

The Question respecting the Depreciation of the Currency, Stated and Examined. 8vo. 1810.

Report on the Depressed State of Agriculture. 8vo. 1821.

Speech upon Colonial Policy and Foreign Commerce. 8vo. 1825.

" upon the Navigation Laws. 8vo. 1825.

" upon the Silk Trade. 8vo. 1826.

" upon the Shipping Interest. 8vo. 1827.

HUTTON (CHARLES, LL.D.)

Royal Military College, Woolwich.

Born August 14, 1737. Appointed Professor of Mathematics at the Royal Military Academy of Woolwich, in November 1774; retired in 1806. Died January 27, 1823.

A Practical Treatise on Arithmetic and Book-keeping. 1764.
A Treatise on Mensuration. 4to. 1771.
Principles of Bridges, and the Mathematical Demonstration of the Laws of Arches. 8vo. 1772.
Mathematical and Philosophical Dictionary. 2 vols. 4to. 1796.
Course of Mathematics. 1798.
Recreations in Mathematics and Natural Philosophy. 4 vols. 8vo. 1803.
Abridgement of the Philosophical Transactions. 18 vols.
Edited an Edition of Robins on Gunnery.
„ the Lady's Diary.
Various Works on Arithmetic, Book-keeping, &c.

HUXLEY (THOMAS HENRY, F.R.S.)

Museum of Practical Geology.

Professor of Palæontology, in the School of Mines.

A History of the Oceanic Hydrozoa. 4to.

Various Contributions to Transactions of the Royal and Linnæan Societies, and to the Journal of Microscopical Science.

IRWIN (EYLES).

East India Company.

Born 1748. Died 1817.

Adventures during a Voyage up the Red Sea and a Journey across the Deserts of Thebes in 1777. With Supplement. 4to. 1780.

Eastern Eclogues.

Epistle to Mr. Hayley.

Ode on the death of Hyder Alley.

An Inquiry into the Feasibility of Buonaparte's Expedition into the East.

Napoleon; or the Vanity of Human Wishes.

JAMES (G. P. R.)

Department of Secretary of State, Foreign.

Born in the year 1801. Appointed British Consul in Norfolk, Virginia, in 1852.

Author of 75 Novels, Tales, &c., the following being the most popular.

Darnley.
Mary of Burgundy.
Henry Masterton.
One in a Thousand.
The Robber.

JEFFREY (FRANCIS, LORD JEFFREY).

Lord Advocate and Lord of Session.

Born October 23, 1773. Educated at the Edinburgh High School, at the University of Glasgow, and at Queen's College, Oxford. Called to the Scottish Bar December 16, 1794. Became Editor of the Edinburgh Review in 1803, having in the previous year, in conjunction with Sydney Smith, Lord Brougham, and Francis Horner, originated it: the first number appeared October 10, 1802; continued Editor till the year 1829; became Lord Rector of the Glasgow University in 1821. Elected M.P. for Perth in 1830, for Malton in 1831, and for the City of Edinburgh in 1832. Appointed Lord Advocate of Scotland in 1832. Raised to the Scottish Bench in 1834, with the title of Lord Jeffrey. Died January 26, 1850.

Selections of Essays from the Edinburgh Review. 4 vols. 1843.
Various Contributions to the Monthly Review.
Edited the Edinburgh Review from 1803 till 1829.

JEREMIE (SIR JOHN).

Department of Secretary of State, Colonial.

Born August 19, 1795. Educated at the Blundell Grammar School, Tiverton. Appointed Chief Justice of St. Lucia, West Indies, in October 1824, and Advocate-General of the Mauritius in 1832; became Puisne Justice of the Supreme Court of Ceylon in 1836. Appointed Governor of Sierra Leone in 1840. Died April 23, 1841.

Essays on Colonial Slavery. 1831.
Recent Events at the Mauritius. 1833.
A Letter on Negro Emancipation and African Civilisation. 1840.

JESSE (EDWARD).

Office of Woods.

Gleanings in Natural History. 3 vols. 8vo. 1832-5.
Anglers' Rambles. 8vo. 1836.

A Summer Day at Hampton Court. 8vo. 1839.
Ditto at Windsor. 12mo. 1841.
Hand-Book to Hampton Court Palace and Gardens. 12mo. 1841.
Scenes and Tales of Country Life. 8vo. 1844.
Anecdotes of Dogs. Cr. 4to. 1846.
Favourite Haunts and Rural Studies. 8vo. 1847.
Hand-Book to Windsor and Eton. 12mo. 1848.
Lectures on Natural History. 8vo. 1861.

JESSE (J. H.)

Admiralty, Whitehall.

Memoirs of the Court of England under the Stuarts. 4 vols. 8vo. 1839–40.
George Selwin and his Contemporaries. 4 vols. 8vo. 1843.
Memoirs of the Pretendents and their Adherents. 2 vols. 8vo. 1845.
Memoirs of the Court of England, 'Hanover.' 3 vols. 1846.
Literary and Historical Memorials of London. 1st and 2nd Series. 8vo. 1847.
London: a Fragmentary Poem. 8vo. 1847.
Richard III. and his Contemporaries. 8vo. 1861.

JUKES (J. B.)

Director of the Ordnance Geological Survey in Ireland.

Voyage of H.M. Ship Fly in Torres Straits. 2 vols. 8vo. 1812.

Excursions in Newfoundland, 1839–40. 2 vols. 8vo. 1842.

Popular Physical Geology. 8vo.

Sketch of the Physical Structure of Australia. 8vo. 1850.

Student's Manual of Geology. 8vo. 1858.

KEITH (THOMAS).

British Museum.

Born 1759. Was Professor of Geography to the Princess Charlotte of Wales in 1814. Subsequently appointed Accountant to the British Museum. Died in 1824.

Plane and Spherical Trigonometry. 8vo. 1801.

A Treatise on the Use of the Globes. 12mo. 1804.

Elements of Geometry. 8vo. 1814.

The Complete Practical Arithmetician.

An Introduction to Geography.

KEMBLE (JOHN MITCHELL).

Lord Chamberlain's Department.

Born in 1807. Educated at the Grammar School, Bury St. Edmunds, and at Trinity College, Cambridge. Held the Office of Examiner and Licenser of Plays under the Lord Chamberlain. Died in 1857.

History of the Saxons in England. 2 vols. 8vo. 1848.
State Papers and Correspondence. 8vo. 1857.
Utility of Antiquarian Collections. 8vo. 1857.
Edited the British and Foreign Quarterly Review.

LAMB (CHARLES).

East India Company.

Born 18 February, 1775. Educated at Christ's Hospital. Appointed to a clerkship in the Accountants' Department, India House, in 1792. Retired in 1825. Died December 27, 1834.

Rosamond Gray. 8vo. 1798.
John Woodville, a Tragedy. 12mo. 1802.
Tales from Shakspeare. 2 vols. 8vo. 1807.
Adventures of Ulysses. 12mo. 1802.

Specimens of English Dramatic Poets, temp. Shakspeare. 8vo. 1808.

Essays and Poems. 2 vols. 12mo. 1818. (The first collected edition.)

Essays of Elia. 8vo. 1823. (Originally published in the London Magazine, 1820–25.)

Album Verses. 8vo. 1830.

Palinque, or the Ancient West, a Poem. 8vo. 1849.

LAMB (SIR JAMES BLAND BURGES, BART., M.P. & D.C.L.)

Foreign Office, Privy Seal Office, and Lord Chamberlain's Department.

Born in the year 1752. Educated for the legal profession at the University of Oxford. Called to the Bar in 1777. Elected M.P. for Helston in 1787. Appointed Under Secretary of State for the Foreign Department and one of the Privy Seal Commissioners in 1789; in 1795 created a Bart. and Knight Marshal of the Royal Household. Died in 1825.

Established and conducted the 'Sun' Evening Newspaper. 1792.

Contributions to the 'Sun' under the Signature Alfred, collected in 1 vol. 8vo. 1792.

Two Vols. of Dramas.

LAYARD (RIGHT HON. H. A., M.P., D.C.L.)

Department of Secretary of State, Foreign.

Born 8th March, 1817. Was attached to the Embassy at Constantinople from 1847 till 1852. Degree of D.C.L. conferred in 1848. Appointed Under Secretary of State for the Foreign Department in February 1852. Elected M.P. for Aylesbury in 1852, and for Southwark in December 1860; reappointed Under Secretary of State for Foreign Affairs in August 1861.

Monuments of Nineveh. 100 plates. Folio. 1848.
Do. Do. 71 plates. Folio. 1853. (Second series.)

Nineveh and its Remains. 2 vols. 8vo. 1848. Fifth edition, 1850.

Discoveries in the Ruins of Nineveh and Babylon, with Travels in Armenia, &c., &c., being the Result of a Second Expedition undertaken for the Trustees of the British Museum. 8vo. 1853.

Various Descriptions of Paintings in Fresco. Imp. 8vo. 1856-7-8-9 and 60.

LEWIS (SIR GEORGE CORNEWALL, BART., M.P.)

Poor Law Board, Board of Control, S. S. Home Treasury, Exchequer, and S. S. War.

Born October 1806. Educated at Eton and Christchurch College, Oxford. Called to the

Bar in 1831. Appointed Poor Law Commissioner in 1839, became Secretary to the Board of Control in November 1847. Was Secretary of State for the Home Department from May 1848 till July 1850; and Financial Secretary to the Treasury from 1850 to 1852. Appointed Chancellor of the Exchequer in May 1855, retained the office till March 1858. Was Secretary of State for the Home Department from June 1859 till July 1861, and Secretary of State for War from July 1861 till date of death in 1863.

Essays on the Use and Abuse of Political Terms. 8vo. 1835.

Remarks on Local Disturbances in Ireland. 8vo. 1836.

Essays on Government of Dependencies. 8vo. 1841.

Influence of Authority in matters of Opinion. 8vo. 1849.

Treatise on Method of Reasoning in Politics. 2 vols. 8vo. 1852.

Enquiry into Credibility of Early Roman History. 2 vols. 8vo. 1855.

Foreign Jurisdiction and the Extradition of Criminals. 8vo. 1859.

Essays on Origin and Formation of Roman Languages. 8vo. 2nd edition. 1862.

Historical Survey of Astronomy of the Ancients. 8vo. 1862.

Fabulæ Æsopæ. 8vo.

Edited the Edinburgh Review from 1853 to 1855.

LISTER (THOMAS HENRY).

Registrar-General of Births, Deaths, and Marriages.

Born in 1801. Died June 1842.

Granby, a novel. 3 vols. 8vo. 1835.
Herbert Lacy, ditto. 3 vols. 8vo.
Arlington, ditto. 3 vols. 1849.
Epicharis, a tragedy.
Life and Administration of Lord Clarendon. 3 vols. 8vo.

LOCKHART (JOHN GIBSON).

Auditor of the Duchy of Lancaster.

Born in the year 1793. Educated at the Glasgow University and at Balliol College, Oxford. Called to the Scottish Bar in 1816. Appointed Auditor of the Duchy of Lancaster in 1843. Edited the Quarterly Review from 1826 till 1853. Died 25 November 1854.

Peter's Letters to his Kinsfolk. 3 vols. 1819.
Valerius: a Roman Story. 3 vols. 8vo. 1821.
Adam Blair: a novel. 8vo. 1822.
Ancient Spanish Ballads. 4to. 1823. (Illustrated edition, 4to. 1841.)

Reginald Dalton: a novel. 3 vols. 1823.
Matthew Wald: a novel. 1 vol. 8vo. 1824.
Life of Robert Burns. 1825.
Life of Sir Walter Scott. 2 vols. 8vo. 1837-39.
Edited the Quarterly Review for 27 years, from 1826 till 1853.

LODGE (EDMUND).

Heralds' College.

Born 1756. Died 1839.

Illustrations of British History: Reigns, Henry VIII. Edward VI., Mary, Elizabeth, and James I. 3 vols. 4to. 1791.
Life of Sir Julius Cæsar. 4to. 1810.
Peerage and Baronetage of Great Britain. 8vo. 1st edition, 1831, continued annually.
Portraits of Illustrious Personages. 4 vols. folio. 1821. 1834.
Genealogy of the British Peerage. Royal 8vo. 1849.

LONG (EDWARD).

Vice-Admiralty Court, Jamaica.

Born 1734. Died 1813.

History of Jamaica or a General Survey of the Ancient and Modern State of that Island. 3 vols. 4to. 1774.

The Prater, a collection of Essays.

The Antigallican: a novel.

Letters on the Colonies, &c.

LYSONS (SAMUEL).

Public Record Department.

Born 17 May 1763. Called to the Bar in 1798. Appointed Keeper of the Records in the Tower in 1803. Died 29 June 1819.

Gloucestershire Antiquities. Folio. 1791.

An Account of Roman Antiquities, discovered at Woodchester, county of Gloucester. Folio. 1797.

Magna Britannia. 1806.

Environs of London, &c. 2 vols. 4to. 1811.

Reliquiæ Britannico-Romanæ. Folio. 1813-17. A collection of Works on Roman Antiquities separately published.

LYTTON (RIGHT HON. SIR EDWARD G. E. LYTTON BULWER, BART., M.P.)

Secretary of State for the Colonies.

Born in the year 1805. Educated at Trinity Hall, Cambridge, graduated B.A. in 1826, and

M.A. in 1835. Elected M.P. for St. Ives in 1831, represented Lincoln from 1832 till 1841. Created a Baronet in 1835. Elected M.P. for Hertfordshire in 1852. Became Rector of the University of Glasgow in 1856. Appointed Secretary of State for the Colonial Department June 1858, resigned June 1859.

Falkland. 8vo. 1825.
O'Neil: or the Rebel. 8vo. 1827.
Pelham. 3 vols. 1828.
Devereux. 3 vols. 1829.
The Disowned. 3 vols. 1829.
Paul Clifford. 3 vols. 1830.
Godolphin. 3 vols. 1831.
Siamese Twins. 1 vol. 1831.
Eugene Aram. 3 vols. 1832.
England and the English. 2 vols. 1833.
The Student (a collection of papers). 2 vols. 1835.
Rienzi. 3 vols. 1835.
The Crisis: a Pamphlet. 1835.
Athens: its Rise and Fall. 2 vols. 1837.
Alice. 3 vols. 1838.
Night and Morning. 3 vols.
Leila: or the Siege of Granada. 8vo. 1838.
Pilgrims of the Rhine. 8vo. 1840.
Zanoni. 3 vols. 1842.
Eva: a Poem. 12mo. 1842.
Last of the Barons. 3 vols. 1843.
Lucretia. 3 vols. 1847.

The New Timon: a Poetical Romance. 8vo. 1846.
A Word to the Public. 1847.
The Last Days of Pompeii. 3 vols.
Confessions of a Water Patient. 1847.
Harold. 3 vols. 1848.
King Arthur: a Poem. 2 vols.
The Caxtons. 3 vols. 1849.
Ernest Maltravers. 3 vols.
Letters to John Bull on Landed Property. 8vo. 1851.
My Novel. 4 vols.
A Strange Story. 2 vols.
What will He Do with It. 4 vols. 1858.

Dramatic Works.

The Lady of Lyons: a Play. 8vo. 1838.
The Sea Captain: a Play. 8vo. 1839.
Richelieu: a Play. 8vo. 1838.
Money: a Comedy. 8vo. 1840.
Not so Bad as we Seem: a Comedy. 8vo.

Edited the New Monthly Magazine in 1841.

LYTTON (EDWARD ROBERT).

Department of the Secretary of State, Foreign.

Eldest son of Sir E. L. Bulwer Lytton, Bart. Appointed Attaché at Washington in 1849, removed to Florence in 1852, and to Paris in

1854; to the Hague in 1855; transferred to St. Petersburgh in 1858, and to Constantinople in the same year; removed to Vienna in 1859. Appointed Consul at Belgrade in 1860. Published under the name of 'Owen Meredith.'

Clytemnestra, and other Poems. 12mo. 1855.
The Wanderer, &c. 12mo. 1859.
Lucile: a Poem. 8vo. 1860.
Serboki Pesme; or National Songs of Servia. 12mo. 1861.

MACAULAY (RIGHT HONOURABLE THOMAS BABINGTON, LORD).

India Board, War Department and Paymaster-General's Office.

Born 25th October 1800. Educated at Trinity College, Cambridge; obtained the Craven Scholarship in 1821, and became Fellow of his College in 1822. Called to the Bar in February 1826, and shortly after appointed a Commissioner in Bankruptcy. Elected M.P. for Calne in 1830, and became Secretary to the Board of Control; returned M.P. for Leeds in 1832, resigned in 1834, received the appointment of Legal Adviser and Member of the Supreme

Council for India; after an absence of three years, employed in drawing up a new Code of India Law, returned to England. Became Secretary at War in 1839. Elected M.P. for Edinburgh in 1840. In 1846 appointed Paymaster-General, with a seat in the Cabinet, in 1849. Elected Lord Rector of the University of Glasgow. Created Baron Macaulay in 1857. Died December 28, 1859.

Pompeii: a Poem. 8vo. 1819.
Evening: a Poem. 8vo. 1821.
Memoirs of the House of Bourbon. 2 vols. 8vo. 1830.
Lays of Ancient Rome. 8vo. 1842.
Critical and Historical Essays, contributed to the Edinburgh Review. 3 vols. 1843.
History of England, from the Accession of James II. 4 vols. 8vo. 1848–55.
Speeches, &c. 8vo. 1831—1853-4.
Various Biographies in the Encyclopædia Britannica and Edinburgh Review.

MACGREGOR (JOHN, M.P.)

Secretary to the Board of Trade.

Report to the British Government on the Commercial Statistics of the Kingdom of the Two Sicilies. Folio. 1840.

Commercial Statistics: a Digest of the Productive Resources; Commercial Legislation, Customs Tariffs; Navigation, Port and Quarantine Laws and Charges, Shipping; Imports and Exports; Money, Weights, Measures, &c., of all Nations. 3 vols. folio. 1844.

MACKENZIE (HENRY).

Comptroller of Taxes, Scotland.

Born in August 1745. Educated at the High School, Edinburgh, and at the Edinburgh University. Appointed Comptroller of Taxes for Scotland in 1804, and retained the office till the date of death, January 14, 1831.

The Man of Feeling: a Novel. 1771
The Prince of Tunis: a Tragedy. 1773
The Man of the World: a Novel. 1783
Julia de Roubigné: a Novel.
The Shipwreck: a Tragedy.
The Force of Fashion: a Comedy.
The White Hypocrite: a Comedy.
Essays in the Mirror and the Lounger.
} Collected and Published together in 8 vols. 8vo. 1808; edited by the Author

An Account of the Proceedings of the Parliament of 1784.

Dramatic Translations. 1 vol. 8vo. 1791.

Various Political Tracts.

McCULLOCH (JOHN RAMSAY).

Comptroller of Her Majesty's Stationery Office.

Born at the Island of Withorn, Wigtonshire, March 1, 1789. Educated by his maternal grandfather, the Rev. Dr. James Laing, and at the Edinburgh University. In 1817 edited the 'Scotsman' Edinburgh Newspaper, and conducted it till 1820. During the years 1820 and 1828 was frequently in London, delivering lectures on Political Economy. In 1828 appointed Professor of Political Economy at the London University; resigned the Professorship in 1832. Appointed Comptroller of Her Majesty's Stationery Office February 20, 1838. Died November 11, 1864.

Discourse on the Rise and Progress and Peculiar Objects of Political Economy. 8vo. 1824.

Principles of Political Economy. 8vo. 1825.

Circumstances which Determine Rate of Wages. 12mo. 1826.

Adam Smith's Wealth of Nations, with Life, Notes, and Introductory Discourse. 4 vols. 8vo. 1828.

Observations on the Duty of Sea-borne Coal, &c. 8vo. 1830. (a Tract.)

Historical Sketch of the Bank. 8vo. 1831.

Influence of the East India Company's Monopoly on Tea. 8vo. 1831.

Dictionary of Commerce. 8vo. 1832. 6th edition, 1859.

Commerce, its Principles and History. 8vo. 1833.

Operation of Duty on Paper. 8vo. 1836.

Statistical Account of the British Empire. 2 vols. 8vo. 1837.

Policy and Probable Consequences of a Repeal of the Corn Laws. 8vo. 1841.

Geographical and Statistical Dictionary of the World. 2 vols. 8vo. 1841.

Treatise on Taxation and the Funding System. 8vo. 1845. 3rd edition, 1863.

The Literature of Political Economy. 8vo. 1845.

A Treatise on the Succession of Property Vacant by Death. 8vo. 1848.

Treatises and Essays on Subjects connected with Political Policy, &c. 8vo. 1853.

Considerations on Partnership with Limited Liability. 8vo. 1856.

A Select Collection of Early English Tracts on Commerce. (Privately printed for the Political Economy Club.)

Contributions to the Edinburgh Review, from 1818 till 1837.

Ditto to the Encyclopædia Britannica.

MACKINTOSH (SIR JAMES, M.P.)

India Company.

Born October 24, 1765. Educated at the University of Aberdeen; from 1784 till 1788 studied for the Medical Profession, when he resigned it. Retired to Brussels and became Foreign Correspondent to the 'Oracle' newspaper. Studied for the law, and was called to the Bar in 1795. Appointed Recorder of Bombay in 1803, and Judge of the Admiralty Court in India 1806. Returned to England in 1812. Elected M.P. for Nairn in 1813, and for Knaresborough in 1819. In 1818 appointed Professor of Law and General Politics in the East India Company's College, Haileybury. Retired from the Professorship in 1824. In 1830 appointed a Commissioner for the Affairs of India. Died May 22, 1832.

The Regency Question. 8vo. 1788.

Vindiciæ Gallicæ: a Defence of the French Revolution, &c., against the Accusations of the Right Hon. Edmund Burke. 8vo. 1791.

Discourse on the Law of Nature and Nations. 8vo. 1799.

Dissertation on the Progress of Ethical Philosophy, chiefly during the 17th and 18th Centuries. 4to. 1830.

History of England, B.C. 55 to A.D. 1572. 3 vols. 1830–32.

Review of the Causes of the Revolution of 1688, &c. 4to. 1834.

View of the Reign of James II. 4to. 1834.

Essays and Reviews published in the Edinburgh Review, &c., collected and published in 3 vols. 8vo.

MADDEN (SIR FREDERICK).

British Museum.

Born in 1801. Appointed to a situation in the British Museum in 1826. Became Assistant-Keeper of Manuscripts in 1828. Knighted in 1832, and appointed Keeper of the Manuscripts in 1837.

Household Book of Queen Mary. 8vo.

The Holy Bible from the Latin Vulgate of Wycliffe. 4 vols. 4to. Edited by Rev. J. Forshall and Sir F. Madden.

Layamon's Brut; or, Chronicle of Britain. 3 vols. 8vo. 1847.

MALCOLM (SIR JOHN, M.P.)

East India Company.

Born in 1769. Appointed to the East India Company's Service at Madras in 1782. After holding various offices under the Company, became Private Secretary to the Governor-General in 1801. In 1803 appointed Governor of Mysore, and in 1809 Minister Plenipotentiary to Persia. Returned to England in 1812. Again went to India in 1817, as Political Agent to the Governor-General. Appointed Governor of Bombay in 1827. Retired in 1830. Elected M.P. for Launceston in 1831. Died May 31, 1833.

Sketch of the Sikhs. Royal 8vo. 1812.
History of Persia, from the most early Period to the Present Time. 2 vols. 4to. 1815.
Memoirs of Central India. 2 vols. 1823.
Political History of India: 1784 to 1823. 2 vols. 8vo. 1826.
Sketches of Persia. 2 vols. 8vo. 1828.
The Administration of British India. 8vo. 1833.
Life of Lord Clive. 3 vols. 1836.

MALMESBURY (JAMES HARRIS, EARL OF).

Department of Secretary of State, Foreign.

Born April 21, 1746. Educated at the Grammar School, Salisbury; at Winchester School; at Merton College, Oxford; and at Leyden. In 1767 appointed Secretary to the

Embassy at Madrid. Elected M.P. for Christchurch in 1770. Was Minister at the Court of Berlin in 1771. In 1777 appointed Ambassador to St. Petersburgh; resigned in 1784. Was Minister at the Hague in 1787; for his services in that capacity, created in 1788 Baron Malmesbury; was Proxy for the Prince of Wales on his marriage with Caroline of Brunswick. Created Earl of Malmesbury, Viscount Fitzharris, in 1800. Died November 20, 1820.

Diaries and Correspondence. 4 vols. 8vo. 1844. Edited by his Grandson.

MALTHUS (THOMAS ROBERT, REV., F.R.S.)

East India Company.

Born in 1766. Educated at the Warrington Academy, and at Jesus College, Cambridge. B.A. in 1788; M.A., 1797. In 1805 appointed Professor of Modern History and Political Economy to the East India Company's College, Haileybury. Died December 29, 1834.

Essay on the Principle of Population. 8vo. 1793. (1st edition.)

Observations on the Effect of the Corn Laws. 8vo. 1814.

Inquiry into the Nature of Rent. 8vo. 1815.

Statement respecting the East India College. 8vo. 1817.

Principles of Political Economy. 8vo. 1820.

The Measure of Value Stated and Illustrated. 8vo. 1823.

Definitions in Political Economy. 8vo. 1827.

Letters, &c. &c.

MARSDEN (WILLIAM, D.C.L., F.R.S.)

India Company and Admiralty.

Born at Verval, County of Wicklow, November 16, 1754. Educated at Trinity College, Dublin. Appointed to a clerkship in the East India Company's Service in 1771. Acted as Sub-Secretary and then as Secretary to the Government at Bencoolen. Returned to England in 1779. Appointed Secretary to the Admiralty in 1795; retired in 1807, with a pension of £1,500 per annum, which he relinquished to the public in 1831. Died October 6, 1836.

History of the Island of Sumatra. 4to. 1783. 3rd edition, 1811.

Dictionary and Grammar of the Malayan Language 4to. 1812.

The Travels of Marco Polo. 4to. 1818.
Numismata Orientalia Illustrata. 2 vols. 4to. 1823-25.
Various Contributions to the Philosophical Transactions and Archæologia.

MARTIN (LEOPOLD CHARLES).

Stationery Office.

Born December 6, 1817. Appointed to a clerkship in Her Majesty's Stationery Office in 1836.

Civil Costumes of England, from the Conquest to George III. 4to. 1842. By L. C. and C. Martin.
The Current Gold and Silver Coins of all Countries; their Weight and Fineness, and their Intrinsic Value in English Money; with Facsimiles of the Coins. By L. C. Martin and C. Trübner. Royal 8vo. 1862. 2nd edition, 1863.

MASSEY (WILLIAM NATHANIEL, M.P.)

Department S. S. Home.

Born in 1809. Educated for the Bar. Elected M.P. for Newport in July 1852, and for Salford in 1857. Was Under-Secretary of State for the Home Department from August 1855 till

March 1858. Appointed Chairman of Committees of the whole House June 1859; resigned in January 1865, upon being appointed Finance Minister for India, in the place of Sir C. E. Trevelyan.

Common Sense *versus* Common Law. 12mo. 1850.
History of England under George III. 3 vols. 8vo. 1855–60.

MERIVALE (HERMAN, C.B.)

Under Secretary of State for India.

Lecture on Political Economy. 8vo. 1837.
Lectures on Colonization and the Colonies. 2 vols. 8vo. 1860.

MERIVALE (JOHN HERMAN).

Court of Bankruptcy.

Born in 1779. Educated at St. John's College, Cambridge. Called to the Bar in 1805. Appointed Commissioner of Bankruptcy in 1831. Died in April 1844.

Chancery Reports, from 1815 to 1817. 3 vols. 8vo.
Collections from the Greek Anthology. 1833.
Poems. 2 vols. 8vo. 1841. (A collected edition.)
Translations of the Minor Poems of Schiller. 8vo. 1844.
Contributions to various Reviews, &c.

MILL (JAMES).

East India Company.

Born April 6, 1773. Educated at the Grammar School, Montrose, and at the Edinburgh University. Intended for the Church; obtained a license to preach in 1798, but relinquished the clerical profession for that of literature. Appointed in 1819 to a situation in the Corresponding Department of the East India Company, and subsequently became head of the department. Died June 23, 1836.

History of British India. 3 vols. 4to. 1818. 5th edition, 10 vols. 8vo. 1858.

Elements of Political Economy. 8vo. 1821.

Analysis of Phenomena of the Human Mind. 2 vols. 8vo. 1829.

Fragment on Sir James Mackintosh. 1835.

Contributions to the Encyclopædia Britannica, under the heads of Colonies, Education, Laws of Nations, and Prison Discipline.

Various Articles in the Edinburgh and London and Westminster Reviews.

MILL (JOHN STUART).

East India Company.

Born in the year 1806. Appointed to a clerkship in the East India Company's Service in 1823, and Examiner of East Indian Correspondence in 1856.

Edited Bentham's 'Rationale of Judicial Evidence,' with Notes, &c. 1827.

A System of Logic, Ratiocinative and Inductive. 2 vols. 8vo. 1843. 5th edition, 1863.

Essays on Unsettled Questions of Political Economy. 8vo. 1844.

Principles of Political Economy. 2 vols. 8vo. 1848. 5th edition, 1863.

Considerations on Representative Government. 8vo. 2nd edition, 1863.

Dissertations and Discussions, Political. 2 vols. 8vo. 1859.

Essay on Liberty. 8vo. 1859.

Thoughts on Parliamentary Reform. 8vo. 1859.

Edited the Westminster Review for some years.

Contributed many Articles to the Edinburgh and Westminster Reviews.

MOLESWORTH (SIR WILLIAM, BART., M.P.)

Office of Works, and Department of S. S. Colonial.

Born in 1810. Educated at Cambridge and Edinburgh. Elected M.P. for East Cornwall in December 1832; for Leeds in 1837, and for Southwark in 1850. Appointed Chief Commissioner of Public Works in January 1853, and Secretary of State for the Colonies in July 1855. Died October 22, 1855.

Edited the Westminster Review, in conjunction with J. S. Mill, from 1835 till 1840.

Edited the Works of Thomas Hobbes. 16 vols. 8vo.

MOORE (THOMAS).

Department of Secretary of State, Colonial.

Born May 28, 1779. Educated at Trinity College, Dublin. Intended for the legal profession; became a Member of the Middle Temple, London. Appointed, in 1804, Treasurer at Bermuda; returned to England shortly after, having appointed a deputy to perform his official duties. Died February 25, 1852.

Odes of Anacreon. 1801.

Lalla Rookh, and other Poems. 4to. 1817.

Irish Melodies. 12mo. 1821.

Memoirs of Captain Rock. 8vo. 1824.

Life of R. B. Sheridan. 2 vols. 8vo. 1825.

Epicurean: a Tale. 12mo. 1827.

Life of Lord Edward Fitzgerald. 2 vols. 8vo. 1831.

Travels of an Irish Gentleman in Search of a Religion. 2 vols. 12mo. 1833.

History of Ireland. 4 vols. 8vo. 1839–46.

Songs, Ballads, Epistles, Odes, &c.

First Collected Edition of Poetical Works. 10 vols. 8vo. 1840–41.

MORIER (JAMES).

Department of Secretary of State, Foreign.

Born in 1780. Appointed British Envoy to the Court of Persia in 1810. Died in 1848.

Travels through Persia, Armenia, Asia Minor, &c. 1812–18. 2 vols. 4to.

Adventures of Hajji Baba. 3 vols. 8vo. 1824.

Ditto ditto in England. 2 vols. 8vo. 1828.

Zohrab, the Hostage. 3 vols. 8vo. 1832.

Ayesha, the Maid of Kars. 3 vols. 8vo. 1834.

Abel Allnutt: a Novel. 3 vols. 8vo. 1837.

The Banished: a Novel. 3 vols. 8vo. 1839.

Mirza: a Romance. 3 vols. 8vo. 1841.
Martin Tourtrond. 8vo. 1849.
Frenchmen in London. 12mo. 1856.

MORTIMER (THOMAS).

Department of Secretary of State, Foreign.

Born in 1730. For some time Vice-Consul in the Netherlands. Died 1809.

The British Plutarch.
A Dictionary of Trade and Commerce. 8vo. 1823.
The Elements of Commerce, Politics, and Finance.
A History of England.
The Student's Pocket Dictionary.

MURCHISON (SIR R. I., F.R.S., D.C.L.)

Museum of Practical Geology.

Born February 19, 1792. Educated at the Durham Grammar School; at the Royal Military College, and at the Edinburgh University. Served in the Army from 1807 till 1815. Appointed Director of the Geological Survey and of the Museum of Practical Geology in 1855. Is M.A. Cambridge and Dublin; D.C.L. Oxford; and Member of the Institute of France.

Silurian System of Geology. 2 vols. 4to. 1839.
Geology of Cheltenham. 8vo. 1845.
Geology of Russia and the Ural Mountains. 2 vols. 4to. 1846.
Siluria; its Rocks and their Foundations. 8vo. 1849.

MURPHY (ARTHUR).

Commissioner in Bankruptcy.

Born December 27, 1730. Educated at the College of St. Omer. Studied for the Bar; became a Member of Lincoln's Inn, and subsequently a Commissioner in Bankruptcy. Died June 18, 1805.

The Gray's Inn Journal. A Weekly Paper. 1752-1754.
Essay on the Life and Genius of Dr. Johnson.
Life and Writings of Miss Ann Elliot. 12mo. 1769.
Translation of Tacitus.
Collected Edition of Works. 7 vols. 8vo. 1786.
Life of David Garrick. 2 vols. 8vo. 1801.
Edited Fielding's Works, with Life, &c.

MUSGRAVE (SIR RICHARD, BART., M.P.)

Collector of Excise, Dublin.

Born 1758. Died April 6, 1818.

History of the Irish Rebellion of 1798. 4to. 1801.

NARES (ROBERT, REV. DR.)

British Museum.

Educated at Westminster School, and at Christchurch College, Oxford. Was Preacher at Lincoln's Inn; Prebend of Lincoln; Archdeacon of Stafford; Canon of Litchfield; Rector of Allhallows, London; and Assistant-Librarian to the British Museum. Died in 1829.

Elements of Orthoepy. 8vo. 1784.
A Chronological View of the Prophecies relating to the Christian Church. 8vo. 1805.
Veracity of the Evangelists Demonstrated. 8vo. 1815.
A Glossary of Words, Phrases, &c., in the Works of English Authors of the age of Elizabeth. 4to. 1822.
Sermons at Lincoln's Inn, &c., &c.
Established, in conjunction with Mr. Beloe, the 'British Critic,' to which he contributed largely.

NEWTON (CHARLES THOMAS, M.A.)

British Museum, and Department of Secretary of State, Foreign.

Educated at Christchurch College, Oxford. Appointed Vice-Consul at Mytelene in January 1852; Consul at Rhodes from 1852 till 1853, and Consul at Rome from June 1859 till January 1861. Appointed Chief of the Department of Oriental Antiquities, British Museum, early in 1861.

Map of British and Roman Yorkshire.

History of the Recent Discoveries at Halicarnassus, Cnidus, and Branchidæ. 2 vols. 8vo. and 1 vol. folio of plates.

ORME (Robert).

East India Company.

Born in 1728. Educated at Harrow. Appointed to the Civil Department of the East India Company; became Member of Council at Fort St. George, and Commissary and Accountant-General. Returned to England in 1758. Died in 1801.

History of the Military Transactions of the British Nation in Hindostan, from 1745 to 1761. 3 vols. 4to. 1763-78.

Historical Fragments of the Mogul Empire of the Mahrattas. 4to. 1805.

A General Idea of the Government and People of Hindostan. 4to. 1811.

History of Savagi (founder of the present nation of Morattoes). 8vo. Privately printed.

OTTLEY (WILLIAM YOUNG, F.R.S.)

British Museum.

Born in 1772. For some time Keeper of the Prints in the British Museum. Died May 26, 1836.

The Origin and Early History of Engraving. 2 vols. 4to. 1816.

The Italian School of Design. 84 Plates. Folio. 1823.

The Florentine School. 54 Plates. Folio. 1826.

Collection of 129 Facsimiles of scarce and curious Prints by the early Masters. 4to. 1826.

Descriptive Catalogue of Pictures in the National Gallery. 8vo. 1826.

A Dictionary of Engravers and their Works. 8vo. 1831.

OWEN (RICHARD, C.B.)

British Museum.

Born in the year 1804. Educated at the Edinburgh University, and studied at St. Bartholomew's Hospital. Is Chief of the Natural History Department, British Museum.

British Fossil Reptilia of the Cretaceous Period. 4to. 1851.

Physiological Series of Comparative Anatomy. 5 vols. 4to. 1833-40.

Odontography; or, Teeth of Animals. 2 vols. 8vo. 1840.

Catalogue of Calculi and other Animal Secretions. 4to. 1842.

Description of the Extinct Gigantic Sloth. 4to. 1843.

Catalogue of Fossil Organic Remains of Mammalia and Birds. 4to. 1845.

History of British Fossil Mammalia and Birds. 8vo. 1846.

Ditto ditto Reptiles. 4to. 1849.

Comparative Anatomy of Invertebrated Animals. 8vo. 1855.

Ditto ditto Vertebrated Animals. 8vo. 1855.

Palæontology: a Summary of Extinct Animals. 8vo. 1861.

And many other Minor Works on Natural History.

PAINE (THOMAS).

Excise Office.

Born January 29, 1737. Appointed to a situation in the Excise 1760; resigned in 1774; removed to America in 1775, and became Editor of the Philadelphia Magazine. In 1781 went on a special mission to France. In 1785 appointed Clerk of the Assembly of Pennsylvania, and received a grant of land and money for his services. On the publication of the Second Part of the Rights of Man, in 1792, was prosecuted by the English Government for libel, and found guilty; was immediately elected Member of the French National Convention for the Department of Calais; remained in France from 1792 till 1802, when he returned to America. Died January 8, 1809.

The American Crisis. 8vo. 1776. 8th edition, 1796.
Common Sense: a Pamphlet. 8vo. 1776.
Various Political Pamphlets (published at Philadelphia, from 1776 till 1783).
Rights of Man, in 2 Parts. 8vo. 1791–2.
Age of Reason, in 2 Parts. 8vo. 1792–5.
Decline and Fall of the System of Finance in England. 8vo. 1796.
Agrarian Justice opposed to Agrarian Law, &c. 8vo. 1797.
Collected Edition of his Works, with Life by Richard Carlile. 2 vols. 8vo. 1819.

PALGRAVE (SIR FRANCIS, K.H.)

Public Record Department.

Born July 1788. Called to the Bar in 1827. Knighted in 1832. In 1833, appointed a Commissioner to enquire into the existing state of the Municipal Corporations of England and Wales. In 1835 became Deputy-Keeper of Public Records. Died July 6, 1861.

Parliamentary Writs and Writs of Military Summons, from 1273 to 1327, &c. 4 vols. folio. 1827–34.

History of England, Anglo-Saxon Period. 18mo. 1831.

Rise and Progress of the English Commonwealth, Anglo-Saxon Period. 2 vols. 4to. 1832.

Rotuli Curiæ Regis, Rolls and Records of the Courts held before the King's Justices. 3 vols. 1835.

The Antient Kalendars and Inventories of His Majesty's Exchequer. 3 vols. 8vo. 1836.

Documents and Records Illustrative of the History of Scotland, &c. 8vo. 1837.

Truths and Fictions of the Middle Ages. 1837.

Reports of the Keeper of the Records, from 1840 to 1861.

History of Normandy and England. 3 vols. 8vo. 1851–57.

The Merchant and the Friar.

Various Letters, Pamphlets, &c., and Contributions to the Quarterly and Edinburgh Reviews.

Hand-Book for Travellers in Northern Italy. (Murray's Series.)

PANIZZI (ANTONIO).

Chief Librarian, British Museum.

Catalogue of the Library of the Royal Society. 8vo. 1839–1841.

Italian Grammar for use of Students in the London University. 8vo. 1828.

Italian Extracts.

Addresses, Letters, &c.

PARKES (JOSEPH).

Court of Chancery.

Born in 1796. Educated at the University of Glasgow. Appointed, in 1833, Secretary to the Royal Commission to enquire into Municipal Corporations. In 1847 became Taxing Master in Chancery.

History of the Court of Chancery. 8vo. 1828.
The Equity and Real Property Laws of the United States of North America. 8vo. 1830.
The Prerogative of Creating Peers. 8vo. 1830.
Charitable Records of Warwick. 8vo.

PENNELL (H. C.)

Admiralty, Whitehall.

Puck on Pegasus. 1860.
Spinning-Tackle, What it is, and Ought to be. 1862.

PLANCHÉ (J. R.)

Heralds' College.

Born February 27, 1796. Appointed Croix Pursuivant of Arms in March 1854.

Lays and Legends of the Rhine. 4to. 1827.
The Descent of the Danube from Ratisbon to Vienna. 8vo. 1828.

History of British Costume. 12mo. 1834.

Regal Records, Coronations of Queens. 12mo. 1838.

The Pursuivant-at-Arms; or History Founded on Facts. 8vo. 1852.

Various Adaptations of Old Plays, &c., for the Modern Stage.

POPE (CHARLES).

Customs.

Born in 1783. Entered the Service of the Customs, March 1800, as a Clerk in the office of the Accountant of Petty Receipts in London. Appointed Warehouse-Keeper at the London Docks, March 1, 1804; and Comptroller of Accounts at Bristol in January 1807. Placed on the Retired List, March 12, 1845.

The Yearly Journal of Trade. 8vo. Published Annually. 1st Edition. 4to. 1835.

PORTER (SIR GEORGE RICHARDSON).

Board of Trade.

Born in 1792. Educated at Merchant Taylors' School. Appointed Chief of the Statistical

Department Board of Trade in 1832, and Joint Secretary in 1846. Died September 3, 1855.

Treatise on Tropical Agriculture. 1833.
Tables of the Revenue, Population, Commerce, &c., from 1820 downwards. 8vo. 1833.
The Effects of Restrictions on the Importation of Corn, &c. 8vo. 1839.
Nature and Properties of the Sugar Cane. 8vo. 1842.
The Progress of the Nation in its various Social and Economical Relations, from beginning of the 19th Century to the Present Time. 3 vols. 8vo. 1836-43.
Treatise on the Manufacture of Porcelain and Glass. 12mo. 1850.
Treatise on the Manufacture of Silk. 12mo. 1850.
Various Contributions to the Statistical Society and British Association Publications.

PORTER (SIR ROBERT KER, K.C.H.)

Department of Secretary of State, Foreign.

Born in 1775. Consul at Venezuela, South America, from July 1835 to November 1842.

The Siege of Acre, relative to the late Scene of Contest in Syria. 8vo. 1801.
Travelling Sketches in Russia and Sweden. 2 vols. 4to, 1809.

A Narrative of the Campaign in Russia in 1812. 4to. 1813.

Travels in Georgiá, Persia, and Armenia, in 1817-20. 2 vols. 4to. 1821–2.

PRAED (WINTHROP MACKWORTH, M.P.)

India Company.

Born July 26, 1802. Educated at Eton and at Trinity College, Cambridge. Called to the Bar in May 1829. Elected M.P. for St. Germains in 1830, and again in 1831. Returned for Great Yarmouth in 1834. Was Secretary to the India Board, under the Ministry of Sir Robert Peel, in 1834 and 1835. Held the offices of Deputy High Steward of the University of Cambridge, and Recorder of Barnstaple. Died July 15, 1839.

Poetical Works, Collected in 2 vols. 8vo. with Preface and Memoir by the Rev. Derwent Coleridge, M.A. Moxon. 1864.

Various Editions of his Poetical Essays and Poems have been published at New York: the 1st in 1844, and a 3rd in 2 vols. in 1855.

PRATT (JOHN TIDD).

National Debt Office.

The History of Savings Banks in England, Wales, Ireland, and Scotland. 8vo. 1842.

PRINGLE (THOMAS).

Register Office, Edinburgh.

Born January 5, 1789. Educated at the Kelso Grammar School, and at the University of Edinburgh. Appointed a clerk in the Public Record Department, Scotland, in 1809. In 1817, established and became editor of the Edinburgh Monthly Magazine, afterwards changed in title to that of 'Blackwood's Magazine.' In 1820, emigrated to the Cape of Good Hope; returned to England in 1826, and became Secretary to the Anti-Slavery Society. Died December 5, 1834.

Edited the Edinburgh Monthly Magazine (now Blackwood's) in 1817.

Account of English Settlers in Albany, South Africa.

Ephemerides; or, Occasional Poems.

Sketches in South Africa.
Teviotdale: and other Poems.
Edited the Friendship's Offering, an Annual.
Collected Edition of his Works, Edited by Leitch Ritchie. 8vo. 1835.

RAFFLES (SIR THOMAS STAMFORD).

East India Company, and Secretary of State's Colonial Department.

Born July 5, 1781. Appointed in 1796 to a clerkship in the Secretary's Department of the India Company; in 1805 transferred to the Under-Secretaryship to the East India Company's Government of Prince of Wales Island, and shortly after to the Chief-Secretaryship. Appointed Lieutenant-Governor of Java in 1811; recalled in 1816. In 1818 became Lieutenant-Governor of Bancoolen, in Sumatra; resigned in 1824. Died in July 1826.

An Essay on the Malay Nation. 1809.
History of Java. 2 vols. 4to. 1817.

REEVES (JOHN).

Alien Office.

Born in 1752. Died 1829.

History of the English Law from the time of the Saxons to Philip and Mary. 4 vols. 1787.

History of the Law of Shipping and Navigation. 8vo. 1792.

History of the Government of the Island of Newfoundland, &c. 8vo. 1793.

Thoughts on the English Government: a Pamphlet. 1795.

REPTON (HUMPHRY).

Household of the Lord-Lieutenant of Ireland.

Born May 2, 1752. Educated at the Grammar Schools of Bury St. Edmunds and Norwich. Appointed, in 1783, Secretary to Mr. Wyndham, when Secretary for Ireland. Died March 24, 1818.

Sketches and Hints on Landscape Gardening. Oblong folio. 1794.

Observations on the Theory and Practice of Landscape Gardening, &c. 4to. 1803.

Odd Whims and Miscellanies. 2 vols. 8vo. 1804.

Observations on the Changes of Taste in Landscape Gardening. 8vo. 1806.

Designs for the Pavilion at Brighton. Folio. 1808.

Variety: a Collection of Essays written in the year 1787. 12mo. 1788.

Collected Edition of Works. Edited by J. C. Loudon. 8vo. 1840.

RICH (CLAUDIUS JAMES).

East India Company.

Born March 28, 1787. Appointed to a clerkship in the East India Company's Service in 1803; and Company's Resident at Bagdad in 1808. Died October 5, 1821.

Memoirs on the Ruins of Babylon. 8vo. 1815-18.
Narrative of a Residence in Koordistan, &c. 2 vols. 8vo. 1836.

RICKMAN (JOHN, F.R.S.)

Clerk-Assistant at the Table of the House of Commons.

Born in 1771. Died in 1841.

Population Returns of Great Britain. 1831.

ROMILLY (SIR SAMUEL, M.P.)

Solicitor-General.

Born March 1, 1757. Called to the Bar in 1783. King's Counsel in 1800. Appointed Solicitor-General in 1806. Elected M.P. for

Queensborough in the same year. Returned M.P. for Westminster in 1818. Died November 2, 1818.

Observations on the Criminal Law of England. 8vo. 1810.
Speeches in Parliament. 2 vols. 8vo. 1820.
Some Anonymous Pamphlets upon Criminal Law.

ROSE (GEORGE).

Board of Trade.

Born in 1744. Died in 1818.

A Brief Examination into the Increase of the Revenue, Commerce, and Navigation of Great Britain.
Considerations on the Debt due by the Civil List.
Observations respecting the Public Expenditure, and the Influence of the Crown.
The Proposed System of Trade with Ireland Explained. A Pamphlet. 8vo. 1787.

RUNNINGTON (CHARLES).

Commissioner for the Relief of Insolvent Debtors.

Born in 1751. Died in 1821.

Edited Hale's History of the Common Law. 2 vols.
Edited Gilbert's Law of Ejectments.
Edited Ruffhead's Statutes at Large. 4 vols. 4to.

RUSSELL (Right Hon. Earl, K.G.)

Treasury and Secretary of State, Home, Colonial, Foreign.

Born 19 August 1792. Educated at Westminster School and at the Edinburgh University. Represented Tavistock in Parliament from 1813 till 1819; Huntingdonshire from 1820 to 1826; Bandon from 1826 to 1830. Appointed Paymaster of the Forces in November 1830. Elected M.P. for Devon in 1831; resigned the Paymaster-Generalship in December 1834. Returned M.P. for Stroud in 1834. Appointed Secretary of State for the Home Department in 1835; transferred to the Colonial Department in August 1839; retired in 1841. Elected M.P. for the City of London in the same year. Appointed First Lord of the Treasury in July 1846; resigned in February 1852. Was Secretary of State for the Foreign Department from December 1852 to February 1853; and President of the Council from June 1854 to January 1855. Appointed Secretary of State for the Foreign Department in June 1859. Created Earl Russell in 1861.

Life of Lord William Russell. 2 vols. 8vo. 1820.

Letters written for the Post and not for the Press. 8vo. 1820.

Don Carlos: a Tragedy. 8vo. 1822.

Nun of Arronca: a Tale. 12mo. 1822.

Essays on History of the English Government. 8vo. 1823.

Memoirs of the Affairs of Europe. 2 vols. 4to. 1824–29.

Establishment of the Turks in Europe. 18mo. 1828.

Essays on Causes of the French Revolution. 8vo. 1832.

Memoirs of Thomas Moore. 8vo. 1852.

Life of C. J. Fox. 2 vols. 8vo. 1859.

Memorials and Correspondence of C. J. Fox. 4 vols. 8vo. 1859.

SCHOMBERG (ISAAC).

Commissioner of the Navy.

Originally a Lieutenant in the Navy; serving under Admirals Rodney and Lord Howe; eventually appointed a Commissioner of the Navy Board. Died in 1813.

Naval Chronology, from the Time of the Romans to the Treaty of Peace. 5 vols. 8vo. 1802.

SCHOMBURGK (ROBERT HERMAN, SIR).

Department of Secretary of State, Foreign.

Born in 1804. Employed from 1831 till 1844 in exploring and surveying some of the Virgin

Islands, and the interior of British Guiana. Was Knighted for his services in 1844. Appointed in May 1848, Consul at St. Domingo, removed to Bangkok in Siam 1857.

A Description of British Guiana. 8vo. 1840.
Views in the Interior of Guiana. Folio. 1841.
History of Barbadoes. Royal 8vo. 1847.

SELLON (BAKER JOHN).

Department of Secretary of State, Home.

Born in 1762. Educated at St. John's College, Oxford. Called to the Bar in 1792. Appointed Police Magistrate in 1815. Died 1835.

Analysis of the Practice of the Court of King's Bench and Common Pleas. 2 vols. 8vo.
Treatise on the Deity and the Trinity. 8vo. 1847.

SHARP (GRANVILLE).

Ordnance Office.

Born in 1734. Appointed to a Clerkship in the Ordnance Office in 1760; resigned in 1770. For many years Chairman of the Association for the Abolition of Negro Slavery. Died in July 1813.

A Representation of the Injustice and Dangerous Tendency of Tolerating Slavery in England. 1769.

Declaration of the People's Natural Rights to a Share in the Legislation. 8vo. 1774.

The Law of Retribution, or a Serious Warning to Great Britain and her Colonies, founded on God's Temporal Vengeance against Tyrant Slaveholders. 8vo. 1776.

Account of the Ancient Division of the English Nation into Hundreds and Tithings, &c. 8vo. 1784.

Remarks on the Uses of the Definite Article in the Greek Testament. 8vo. 1798.

Three Tracts on the Syntax and Pronunciation of the Hebrew Tongue. 8vo. 1804.

Case of Saul, showing that his Disorder was a real Spiritual Possession, &c. 8vo. 1807.

A Short Treatise on the English Tongue.

Remarks on the Prophecies.

Treatise on Duelling.

Declaration on the Law of Nature and Principles of Action in Man.

SHEIL (RICHARD L., RIGHT HON., M.P.)

Board of Trade, Mint, Greenwich Hospital, &c.

Born in 1794. Educated at the Jesuit College of Stonyhurst and at Trinity College, Dublin. Called to the Irish Bar in 1814. Elected M.P. for Milborne Port in 1829, and for County Louth in 1831. Appointed in 1838 a Commissioner of Greenwich Hospital; in 1839 became Vice-President of the Board of Trade and a Member of the Privy Council. Appointed Judge Advocate-General in June 1841, and in 1846 Master of the Mint; retired in 1850, and went as Minister at the Court of Tuscany. Died May 23, 1851.

Adelaide: a Tragedy.
The Apostate: a Tragedy.
Ballamira: a Tragedy.
Evadne: a Tragedy.
The Huguenot: a Tragedy.
Various Articles in the New Monthly Magazine, when edited by T. Campbell.

SHERIDAN (RICHARD BRINSLEY, RIGHT HON.)

Department of Secretary of State, Foreign, and Navy Office.

Born in September 1751. Educated at Dublin and Harrow School. Elected M.P. for Stafford in 1780. Appointed Under-Secretary of State for Foreign Affairs in 1782; became Treasurer of the Navy, and Privy Councillor in 1806. Elected M.P. for Westminster in the same year. Died July 7, 1816.

The Rivals. 1775.
The Duenna. 1775.
The School for Scandal. 1777.
Trip to Scarborough. 1777.
The Critic. 1779.
Pizarro. 1799. And other Dramatic Works.
A Translation of Aristænetus.
A Letter to Henry Dundas, &c.

SINCLAIR (JOHN, SIR, BART., M.P.)

Board of Agriculture, Scotland, &c.

Born in 1754. Admitted an Advocate in Scotland 1775. Elected M.P. for Caithness in 1780. Called to the English Bar in 1782. Created a Baronet in 1786. Appointed President of the Board of Agriculture, Scotland, in 1793; made a Privy Councillor in 1810. Died December 21, 1835.

History of the Revenue of Great Britain. 3 vols. 4to. 1785–1789–1790.
A Statistical Account of Scotland, drawn up from the Communication of the Ministers of the different Parishes. 21 vols. 8vo. 1791–99.

Thoughts on the Naval Strength of Great Britain.
Considerations on Militias and Standing Armies.
The Code of Health and Longevity. 4 vols. 8vo. 1807.
Husbandry of Scotland. 2 vols. 8vo. 1812.
Essays on Agriculture, including Observations on Gardening, &c. 8vo. 1819.
An Account of the Northern Districts of Scotland.
Papers on the Bullion Question.
The Originals of the Ossianic Poëms, with a Dissertation.
Many other Works on Finance and Agriculture.

SLEEMAN (WILLIAM HENRY, SIR, K.C.B.)

East India Company.

Born in 1788. Appointed a Cadet in the East India Company's service in 1808. Became Agent in the Saugur and Nurbudda District in 1820. Appointed to the Residency at Lucknow in 1849. Died February 10, 1856.

Military Discipline in our Indian Army.
Treatise on Political Economy.
Review and Analysis of the Peculiar Doctrines of the System of Political Economy founded by Ricardo.
Rambles and Recollections of an Indian Officer. 1843.
Diary in Oude. 1852.

SMITH (JAMES).

Ordnance Office.

Born February 10, 1775. Educated at a private school at Chigwell; articled to his Father, who was Solicitor to the Ordnance Office, and was subsequently appointed to the same office. Died December 24, 1839.

Rejected Addresses. 12mo. 1812.
'At Home,' written for Charles Mathews the elder.
Various Contributions to the London Review, New Monthly Magazine, &c.

SMITH (JOHN THOMAS).

British Museum.

Born June 23, 1766. Appointed Keeper of the Prints in the British Museum in 1816. Died March 8, 1833.

Antiquities of London and its Environs. 4to. 1791–1800.
Remarks on Rural Scenery. 4to. 1797.
The Rag and Bob-Tail, or Portraits of Notorious Personages, temp. Cromwell. 4to. 1800.
Antiquities of Westminster. 4to. 1807.
Ancient Topography of London. 4to. 1815.

Vagabondiana, or Remarkable Beggars, &c. 4to. 1815–17.

Nollekens and his Times. 2 vols. 8vo. 1815.

Cries of London. 4to. 1839.

Book for a Rainy Day, or Recollections for Fifty Years. 8vo. 1845.

Antiquarian Rambles in the Streets of London. 2 vols. 8vo. 1846.

SPENCER (WILLIAM ROBERT, THE HON.)

Commissioner of Stamps and Taxes.

Born in 1770. Educated at Harrow and at Oxford. Died in 1834.

Translation of 'Bürger's Leonore,' with Illustrations by Lady Diana Beauclerc. 1796.

Various Poetical Works.

STAUNTON (GEORGE LEONARD, SIR, BART.)

Department of Secretary of State, Foreign.

Born April 19, 1737. Educated at the College of Montpellier in France, and obtained a Medical Degree in 1760. Practised in the West Indies from 1763 till 1770, as a Physician; relinquished the Medical Profession for that of Law, and became Attorney-General of the West India Island of Granada. In 1780 appointed Private Secretary to Lord Macartney when Governor of Madras; was created a Baronet for his services in India. In 1792 appointed, in conjunction with Lord Macartney, Minister Plenipotentiary to the Court of China. Died January 14, 1801.

Notes and Proceedings during the British Embassy to Pekin. 2 vols. 4to. 1797.
Narrative of Chinese Embassy to the Tartars in 1712-15. Translated from the Chinese. 8vo. 1821.
Miscellaneous Notices Relating to China. 8vo. 1822.
Ta Tsing Lew Lu, the Fundamental Laws of China.
Remarks on the British Relations with China and the Proposed Plans for Improving them. 8vo. 1830.

STEPHEN (JAMES, SIR, K.C.B.)

Department of Secretary of State, Colonial.

Born January 3, 1789. Educated at Trinity Hall, Cambridge. Called to the Bar in 1812; made Counsel to the Colonial Office in 1813; appointed Assistant Under-Secretary for the Colonies in 1833, and Under-Secretary of State in 1836; retired in 1847. Died September 14, 1859.

Essays on Ecclesiastical Biography. 2 vols. 8vo. 1849, Originally published in the Edinburgh Review.

Lectures on the History of France. 2 vols. 8vo. 1851.

STEPHEN (JAMES, M.P.)

Court of Chancery.

Educated at Winchester School; followed the Legal Profession, and was for some time Parliamentary Reporter to the 'Morning Chronicle' Newspaper; held an office in the Prize Court, at St. Kitts; on his return to England in 1807 elected M.P. for Tralee. Appointed Master in Chancery in 1812. Died in 1832.

War in Disguise, or the Frauds of Neutral Flags: a Pamphlet. 8vo. 1806.

The Slavery of the British West Indian Colonies Delineated, &c. 2 vols. 8vo. 1824-30.

England Enslaved by her own Slave Colonies. 8vo. 1826.

ST. JOHN (SPENCER).

Department of Secretary of State, Foreign.

Employed as Secretary to Sir J. Brooke at Borneo in 1848, and at Siam in 1850; held various appointments in Siam and Borneo from 1851 till 1855. Appointed Charge d'Affaires and Consul-General at Hayti in 1861.

Life in the Forests of the Far East. 2 vols. 1862.

STUART (JAMES, OF DUNEARN).

Office of Inspectors of Factories.

Born in 1776. Educated for the Legall Profession; became a Writer to the Signet in 1798. In 1830 was Editor of the 'Courier' Newsppaper. Appointed Inspector of Factories in 1835. Died in 1849.

Three Years in North America. 2 vols. 8vo. 1829.
For some time Editor of the 'Courier' Newspaper.

SYDENHAM (C. E. POULETT THOMSON, LORD).

Board of Trade and S. S. Colonial.

Born September 13, 1799. Elected M.P. for Dover in 1826. Appointed Vice-President of the Board of Trade and Treasurer of the Navy in 1830. Elected M.P. for Manchester in 1832.

Became President of the Board of Trade in June 1834; and in 1839 appointed Governor-General of Canada, and created Baron Sydenham. Died September 19, 1841.

Speech on Moving the Appointment of a Select Committee to Inquire into the State of the Taxation of the United Kingdom. 8vo. 1830.

TALFOURD (THOMAS NOON, SIR).

Court of Common Pleas.

Born January 26, 1795. Educated at the Reading Grammar School, and with Mr. Chitty, the Special Pleader. Called to the Bar in 1821. Appointed Sergeant at Law in 1833. Returned M.P. for Reading in 1835, and again in 1847. Appointed one of the Justices of the Court of Common Pleas in July 1849. Died March 14, 1854.

Ion: a Tragedy. 8vo. 1835.
Letters of Charles Lamb, with a Sketch of his Life. 8vo. 1837.
The Athenian Captive: a Tragedy. 8vo. 1838.
A Proposed New Law of Copyright, &c. 8vo. 1838.
Glencoe: a Tragedy. 8vo. 1839.

Vacation Rambles and Thoughts in 1841–42-43. 8vo. 1844. (Supplement, 1854.)

Recollections of a First Visit to the Alps in 1841. 8vo. (privately printed.)

Final Memorials of Charles Lamb, comprising his unpublished Letters. 2 vols. 1843.

The Castilian: a Tragedy. 1853.

Various Political Pamphlets.

Parliamentary Speeches.

TAYLOR (TOM).

Local Government Acts Office.

Born in 1817. Educated at the Sunderland Grammar School, at the Glasgow University, and at Trinity College, Cambridge. Called to the Bar in 1845. Appointed Assistant-Secretary to the Board of Health (now Local Government Acts Office) in 1850; became Secretary in 1854.

Biography of Thomas Clarkson. 12mo. 1839.

Autobiography of B. R. Haydon, the Painter. 3 vols. 8vo. 1853.

Local Government and Public Health Acts, 1858. 12mo. 1858.

Autobiographical Recollections of C. R. Leslie, R.A. 2 vols. 8vo. 1860.

Pictures in the International Exhibition of 1862. 12mo.
Various Dramatic Works.
Contributions to Punch.

TENNENT (JAMES E., SIR, LL.D.)

Board of Trade, &c.

Born April 7, 1804. Educated at Trinity College, Dublin. Called to the Bar in 1831. Elected M.P. for Belfast in 1832-1835 and 1841. Appointed Secretary to the India Board in September 1841; was Civil Secretary to the Government of Ceylon from July 1845 to December 1850; Secretary to the Poor Law Board from February to November 1852. Elected M.P. for Lisburn in the same year; became Joint-Secretary to the Board of Trade in November 1852.

Travels in Greece in 1825.
Letters from the Ægean. 2 vols. 8vo. 1829.
History of Modern Greece. 2 vols. 8vo. 1830.
Travels in Belgium. 2 vols. 8vo. 1841.
Copyright of Designs for Printed Fabrics. 8vo. 1841.
Progress of Christianity in Ceylon. 8vo. 1850.
Wine, its Use and Taxation. 8vo. 1855.
Account of the Island of Ceylon. 2 vols. 8vo. 1860. 5th edition.
Sketches of the Natural History of Ceylon. 8vo. 1861.

TENTERDEN (CHARLES ABBOTT, LORD).

Lord Chief Justice of the King's Bench.

Born October 7, 1762. Died November 4, 1832.

A Treatise of the Law Relating to Merchant Ships and Seamen. 8vo. 1802.

THOMS (W. J., F.S.A.)

House of Lords.

Born November 10, 1803. Originally a clerk in the Secretary's office, Chelsea Hospital; transferred to the House of Lords, as one of the Clerks of Printed Papers; is now Assistant Librarian.

A Collection of Early Prose Romances. 3 vols. 8vo. 1828.

Lays and Legends of Various Nations. 8vo. 1834.

Book of the Court. 8vo. 1838.

Anecdotes and Traditions. 8vo. 1839.

Stow's Survey of London, with Notice of Life and Writings. 12mo. 1842.

Caxton's 'Reynard the Fox.' 1844.

Translation of Worsaae's Primeval Antiquities of Denmark. 8vo. 1849.

Edited 'Notes and Queries,' from commencement in November 1849.

TREVELYAN (SIR CHARLES E., K.C.B.)

East India Company, and Treasury.

Born in 1807. Educated at the Chester-House School, and Haileybury College. Appointed Writer in the East India Company's Service in October 1826; acted as Deputy-Secretary to the India Government in the Secret and Political Department from 1831 till 1836, and Secretary to the Sudder Board of Revenue from 1836 to 1838. Appointed Assistant-Secretary to the Treasury in January 1840; made Governor of Madras in January 1859; recalled in May 1860. Appointed Member of Council for India, and successor to Mr. Lang as Finance Minister in November 1862.

A Report on the Inland Customs and Town Duties of the Bengal Presidency. 1 vol. 8vo. 1835.
On Education of the People of India. 8vo. 1838.
Irish Crisis. (Published in the Edinburgh Review.) 1848.
Application of Roman Letters to the Languages of Asia. 8vo. 1854.
Statement of Circumstances connected with the Recall of Sir C. E. Trevelyan. 8vo. 1860.

TROLLOPE (ANTHONY).

General Post Office.

Macdermots of Ballycloran. 3 vols. 8vo. 1847.

Kellys and the O'Kellys. 3 vols. 8vo. 1848.
La Vendée. 3 vols. 8vo. 1850.
Warden. 8vo. 1855.
Three Clerks. 3 vols. 8vo. 1857.
Doctor Thorne. 3 vols. 8vo. 1858.
Castle Richmond. 3 vols. 8vo. 1859.
Bertrams. 3 vols. 1859.
Barchester Towers. 3 vols. 1859.
Framley Parsonage. 3 vols. 1860.
North America. 2 vols. 8vo. 1861.
Orley Farm. 2 vols. 8vo. 1862.
Tales of All Countries. 2 vols. 1862.

TURNER (SAMUEL).

East India Company.

Born in 1759. Died January 2, 1802.

An Account of an Embassy to Thibet. 8vo. 1800.
Various Contributions to the Transactions of the Asiatic Society.

TURNER (THOMAS HUDSON).

Record Office.

Born in 1814. Died June 17, 1852.

Domestic Architecture of the Middle Ages. 4 vols. 1851.

Early Household Expenses. (Edited for the Roxburgh Club.)

Various Papers in the Athenæum, Archæological Journal, &c.

TWISS (HORACE, M.P.)

Secretary of State, Colonial Department, Duchy of Lancaster, &c.

Called to the Bar in 1811. Elected M.P. for Wootton Bassett in 1820. Appointed Under-Secretary of State for the Colonies in 1828, and Vice-Chancellor of the Duchy of Lancaster in 1844.

Life of Lord Eldon. 3 vols. 8vo. 1844.
Various Dramatic Works and Poems.

TYTLER (ALEXANDER FRAZER, LORD WOODHOUSELEE).

Lord Advocate of Scotland and Commissioner of Justiciary.

Born October 15, 1747. In 1770 admitted Advocate; in 1786 appointed Professor of History to the Edinburgh University. Obtained the office of Judge-Advocate of Scotland in 1790. Created a Lord of Session, under the title of Lord Woodhouselee, in 1802. Appointed Lord of Justiciary in 1811. Died January 4, 1813.

Outlines of a Course of Lectures on Universal History. 8vo. 1782.
An Essay on the Principles of Translation. 8vo. 1791.
A Treatise on Martial Law. 8vo. 1800.
Elements of General History, Ancient and Modern. 2 vols. 8vo. 1801.
Memoirs of the Life and Writings of Lord Kaimes. 2 vols. 4to. 1807.
An Historical and Critical Essay on the Life of Petrarch. 8vo. 1810.
Universal History from the Creation to beginning of the 18th Century. 6 vols. 8vo. 1834.
Decisions of the Court of Session.

VAUX (W. S. W.)

British Museum. Department of Coins and Medals.

Sketch of Ancient Assyria and Persia. 8vo. 1850.
Hand-Book to Antiquities in the British Museum. 8vo. 1851.
Nineveh and Persepolis Described. 8vo. 1855.

WARD (ROBERT PLUMER, M.P.)

Department of Secretary of State, Foreign; Admiralty; Ordnance, and Treasury.

Born March 19, 1765. Educated at Christchurch, Oxford. Called to the Bar in 1790. Elected M.P. for Cockermouth in 1802. Was Under-Secretary of State for the Foreign Department, from January 1805 till February 1806; a Lord of the Admiralty from 1807 till 1811; Clerk of the Ordnance from 1811 till 1823, when he was appointed Auditor of the Civil List. Died August 13, 1846.

Inquiry into the Foundation and History of the Law of Nations in Europe, from the Greeks to the Age of Grotius. 1795.

An Inquiry into the Conduct of European Wars. 8vo. 1803. (A Pamphlet.)

Tremaine: a Novel. 3 vols. 8vo. 1825.

De Vere; or, the Man of Independence: a Novel. 3 vols. 8vo. 1827.

Illustrations of Human Life. 1837.

Historical Essay on the Revolution of 1688. 2 vols. 8vo. 1838.

Pictures of the World at Home and Abroad. 3 vols. 8vo. 1839.

De Clifford: a Novel. 4 vols. 8vo. 1841.

Chatsworth: a Romance of a Week. 3 vols. 8vo. 1844

WATERHOUSE (G. R.)

British Museum, Department of Geology.

Natural History of Mammalia. 2 vols. 8vo. 1846–49.

WATTS (Alaric A.)

Office of Inland Revenue.

Born March 16, 1799. Died April 1864.

Poetical Sketches. 12mo. 1822.
Poetical Album. 8vo. 1828–29.
Scenes of Life and Shades of Character. 8vo. 1831.
Lyrics of the Heart, and other Poems. 8vo. 1851.
Edited the 'Literary Souvenir' from 1825 till 1834. 10 vols. 8vo.
Edited the 'Leeds Intelligencer' Newspaper, the 'Manchester Courier,' and the 'Standard' Evening Newspaper.

WILKINS (Sir Charles, F.R.S., D.C.L.)

East India Company.

Born in 1759. Appointed to a Writership in the East India Company's Service in 1770; returned to England in 1786; became Librarian to the East India Company in 1801, and in

1805 Visitor and Examiner in the Oriental Department at Addiscombe and Haileybury. Knighted in 1833. Died May 15, 1836.

Various Translations of Sanskrit Literature. 1784-1786.
Edited Richardson's Dictionary of the Persian and Arabic Languages. 2 vols. 4to. 1806.
Grammar of the Sanskrit Language. 4to. 1808.

WILSON (JAMES).

East India Company, and the Treasury.

Born in 1805. Elected M.P. for Westbury in 1847. Appointed Secretary to the Board of Control in 1848; and in 1852 Financial Secretary to the Treasury. Elected M.P. for Devonport in 1857. Nominated Finance Minister for India in 1859. Died, at Calcutta, August 11, 1860.

Influences of the Corn Laws, &c. 8vo. 1839-40.
Fluctuations of Currency, Commerce, &c., Referable to the Corn Laws. 8vo. 1840.
Essays on Capital, Currency and Banking. 8vo. 1847.
Established and Edited the 'Economist' Newspaper in 1843.

WORDSWORTH (WILLIAM).

Stamp Office.

Born April 7, 1770. Educated at the Grammar School of Hawkshead, Lancashire, and at St. John's College, Cambridge. In 1813 appointed Distributor of Stamps for Westmoreland; retired with a pension in 1842, and became Poet Laureate in 1843. Died April 23, 1850.

An Evening Walk and Descriptive Sketches. 4to. 1793.
Lyrical Ballads. 12mo. 1798. 2nd edition, in 2 vols., 1800.
The Excursion. 4to. 1814.
The White Doe of Rylstone. 4to. 1815.
Peter Bell, and The Waggoner. 1819.
Yarrow Revisited. 12mo. 1835.
Collected Edition of Works. 7 vols. 8vo. 1842.
Prelude on the Growth of a Poet's Mind. 8vo. 1850.
Poems of Early and Late Years.
Sonnets, Odes, &c.

WORSLEY (SIR RICHARD, BART., M.P.)

Lord Chamberlain's Department.

Born in 1751. For many years M.P. for Newport, Isle of Wight; was Comptroller of the

Household to George III.; and Governor of the Isle of Wight. Died in 1805.

History of the Isle of Wight. 4to. 1781.
Musæum Worslianum, with views of Places in the Levant, taken in the years 1785–6–7. 2 vols. folio. 1803.

WRAXALL (SIR NATHANIEL WILLIAM, BART.)

East India Company.

Born April 8, 1751. Appointed to the Civil Service of the East India Company in 1769. Acted as Judge-Advocate and Paymaster in the Expedition against Guzeret in 1771; returned to Europe in 1772. Obtained a Seat in Parliament in 1780. Created a Baronet in 1813. Died November 7, 1831.

Cursory Remarks made in a Tour through some of the Northern Parts of Europe. 8vo. 1775.
Memoirs of the Kings of France of the Race of Valois. 2 vols. 8vo. 1777.
History of France under the Race of Valois, from 1364 to 1574. 2 vols. 1785.

History of France from 1574 to 1610. 3 vols. 4to. 1795.
Memoirs of Courts of Berlin, Dresden, &c., in the years 1777–8–9. 2 vols. 8vo. 1799.
Tour Round the Baltic, through the Northern Countries of Europe. 8vo. 1807.
Historical Memoirs of My Own Time, from 1772 to 1784. 3 vols. 8vo. 1815.

YATES (E. H.)

General Post Office.

After Office-Hours. 12mo. 1861.
Broken to Harness. (Published in the 'Temple Bar' Magazine.)

YOUNG (ARTHUR).

Board of Agriculture, Scotland.

Born September 7, 1741. For many years Secretary to the Board of Agriculture, Scotland. Died April 12, 1820.

Agricultural and Statistical Tour through the Southern Counties, &c. 8vo. 1768.
A Six Months' Tour through the North of England, &c. 4 vols. 8vo. 1771.

A Farmer's Tour through the East of England. 4 vols. 8vo. 1770-71.

Tour in Ireland. 2 vols. 8vo. 1780.

Travels during the years 1787-8-9 and 90. 2 vols. 4to. 1794.

The Farmer's Letters to the People of England. 2 vols. 1768-71.

The Farmer's Guide in Hiring and Stocking Farms. 2 vols. 8vo. 1770.

Rural Economy; or, Essays on the Practical Part of Husbandry. 8vo. 1770.

A Course of Experimental Agriculture. 2 vols. 4to. 1770.

Political Arithmetic, &c. 8vo. 1774.

The Farmer's Kalendar. 8vo. Commenced in 1800.

Essay on Manures. 8vo. 1804.

Advantages which have Resulted from the Establishment of the Board of Agriculture. 8vo. 1809.

Inquiry into the Progressive Value of Money, as Marked by the Price of Agricultural Produce. 8vo. 1812.

Edited 'Annals of Agriculture.' 45 vols. Commenced in 1784.

YOUNG (Sir William, M.P.)

Department of Secretary of State, Colonial.

Born in 1750. Educated at Eton, Cambridge, and Oxford. Elected M.P. for St Mawes in

1783. For some time Governor of Tobago. Died in 1815.

History of Athens. 8vo. 1777.
The West India Common-Place Book. 4to. 1807.
The Rights of Placemen.
Edited Dr. Brook Taylor's 'Contemplatio Philosophica.'